Lana's Magic Garden

by
Lana Stevens

Edited by
Gary Dowell

Art Design by
Lana Stevens

1st Artist
Nick Stevens

2nd Artist
Geraldine Connon

Copyright © 2003

ISBN# 0-9714206-0-2

Library of Congress Control Number: 2003094741

Fire & Ice Publishing Enterprises
14255 Preston Rd., Ste. 831
Dallas, TX 75240

All rights reserved. The text of this publication, or any part there of, may not be reproduced in any manner whatsoever without written permission from the publisher.

Introduction

I felt the need to express my psychic ability and experiences and try to help others achieve for themselves. For the people to understand positive and negative of magic. I find that my clients are always asking questions. For example, how long have I been a psychic. How did I know I was a psychic? What is the extent of my ability. What are the difference between white, gray and black magic? I try to help them make wise choices based on their decisions before they enter into magic. To try to understand the law of averages and what rules mother nature. I also discuss parts about different religions and beliefs. I explain that its doesn't depend on your religious background that determines whether or not to end up in hell. I also discuss the waxing moon, the waning moon, the black moon. The new moon and what the magical properties are. I also explore and discuss about the planets. I go beyond that and express my opinion about the elements (air, earth, wind, fire). The different stones and the power they have or don't have. How chandeliers will do magical powers as well. I find them to be very cleansing and sudding, as they have worked in homes and hotels for the longest time. They absorb lots of negative energy; perhaps this is why you feel good in a five star hotel.

May you enjoy this book as a guide in life. Bless it be. Lana.

Lana's Magic Garden

Page 1 To Banish Negativity Into The Woods

Page 2 The rest of banishing negativity into the woods

Page 3 Figure candles; what they are and how to use them. Which colors do what.

Page 4 The spinster lady

Page 5 The witch

Page 6 The great spook that happens to be real.

Page 7 Crossing over

Page 8 And coming back

Page 9 Why do people go to psychics?

Page 10 The cat candles

Page 11 One love potion, pink carnations and wine.

Page 12 The hair ritual

Page 13 More potions and spells- how to do them

Page 14 The mirror box.

Page 15 What the mirror box should look like. The bag and candles.

Page 16 Candles help. To use them and what they can do.

Page 17 Keeping your lover faithful spell.

Page 18 More candles and what they do

Page 19 Sin Eating

Page 20 Cemetery

Page 21 Oils and the purpose....what they can do.

Page 22 More about oils.

Page 23 Kitchen stock

Page 24 Stones, herbs and root...in bulk, preferably.

Page 25 Stones and what magic powers they possess.

Page 26 Waxing moon, new full moon, waning moon

Page 27 Chakra balancing

Page 28 Planets

Page 29 The body is just an instrument.

Page 30	Miracles
Page 31	About miracles
Page 32	The Powers of God, Mother May and Saint Ann working in mysterious ways
Page 33	Picture of God taken at St. Anne de Beaupre's Church in old Quebec
Page 34	More miracles
Page 35	When God steps in to help you
Page 36	Magic plants and flowers
Page 37	Hollywood's ghost story
Page 38	Continuing Hollywood's ghost story
Page 39	About past life regression and time travel
Page 40	The self conscious mind and putting your priorities in perspective.
Page 41	The Chinese Zodiac
Page 42	The rest of the Chinese Zodiac
Page 43	The treasures of May Dew
Page 44	Attract love with colors
Page 45	Gardens are very enchanting
Page 46	Wishbone
Page 47	Lana's first spell
Page 48	Superstition
Page 49	The itchy hand
Page 50	The evil eye
Page 51	Psalm 70
Page 52	Olden days of Salem
Page 53	To Advertise for a husband....New Orleans style
Page 54	Old antiques and estate sales
Page 55	All about dream magic
Page 56	Epidemic in New Orleans
Page 57	The art of yoga is a spiritual thing
Page 58	Invoking the elements
Page 59	Self conscious mind...dressing for what you want.

Page 60	Karma
Page 61	The feast of Saint Anne
Page 62	The Redbluff Story
Page 87	Lana's Home
Page 100	Pots and Pans

To Banish Negativity Into The Woods

Step 1: Take the sage and make a circle.

Step 2: Have the person enter the circle and sit in a cross-legged position. Place a chopping board on the table close to you. Anoint yourself with the master oil and peace oil (a little uncrossing oil wouldn't hurt, for extra protection).

Step 3: Put a generous amount of uncrossing oil on the wrist and forehead of the person you are going to cleanse. Have them rub their wrists together, and then rub them down the sides of their neck.

Step 4: Take a piece of their hair and some fingernail or toenail, and place it in a small frying pan. Add two large tablespoons each of frankincense and myrrh, one dram of uncrossing oil (two if very bad), a tablespoon of jinx removing powder and a tablespoon of dragon blood. You can also add about two tablespoons of van van incense powder or John the Conqueror powder.

Step 5: Say the chant as you walk around the person with the frying pan (be sure to stay outside the circle). As you go, light the frying pan with matches. Have a pot holder handy, just in case the frying pan starts to get hot. You'll be going from the top to the bottom of the person (from the head to the toes) as you walk around them. When you're halfway done, blow out the flames and then cast them out the door. Rebuke them into the darkness, out into the woods: "I rebuke you bad spirits. In the name of Jesus, I bind you."

Step 6: Once the chant is over, place the white candle in the person's hand and have them say their name-first and last- three times. Take the candle and walk around the person from toe to toe while saying the chant of the white light. Place the white candle on the table (or alter, if you have one) and snuff (never blow) it out.

Step 7: Take the blue candle and place it in the person's hand. Have them say their name- first and last- three times. Take the candle and walk around the person from toe to toe while saying the chant of the blue light (go around the person about two or three this time). Place it on the table or alter, and snuff it out as well.

Page 2

Step 8: Stand in front of the person and pull them out of the circle. Now they are cleansed. If they look in the mirror, they will see themselves glowing and shining with happiness. Pick up the sage and throw it away; the person has been cleansed and cannot go back into the circle. Throw out the contents of the frying pan, as well.

If the person steps back inside the circle, you must repeat the process. To do so is very, very bad luck. The person who performed the ritual must now wash out the frying pan and put frankincense and myrrh in it to flush the negativity from the house and do another chant.

"I rebuke and bind Satan in the name of God, and I cast him out of this house, back into the woods. You shall go back into the darkness. Into the rocks in the wilderness you go, far away from us. I send you to hell and I rebuke and bind you in the name of Jesus. Go away, Satan, you are not wanted here. Into the darkness you go, and will remain there. Amen.

One famous love ritual is the red dolls candles. The candles face one another to make two people come together. You inscribe each one on the inside with the name-first and last- of the persons who are to come together. You have now dedicated the candles to one another. Put some red rose oil on them. On the parchment paper, make a drawing of a heart. Write the names on it in dove's blood or dragon's blood ink. Place the candles on the drawing, and will them together with your mind. The more energy you give them, the faster they will work. Do not allow negativity to enter, as this will weaken the work. Your will and projection is everything. Let the candles burn for as many hours as possible, for as long as seven days before snuffing them out. Snuff out daily, never leave them unattended.

When using the candles, face them away from one another, in other words. Back-to-back is to break them up. Be careful, or you might have to deal with karma, unless the one you are trying to separate was yours first. Then it's a different situation, and falls under "Mother sworn to protect her home..."

Candle Figure: Male or Female. Color pink candles are used for attracting friendship or to obtain affection from one's family.

Candle Figure: Male or Female. Color brown candles are used to restore qualities which have been weakened or destroyed, such as male potency or female passions.

Candle Figure: Male or Female. Color white candles pertain to purity, spirituality, obtaining a goal such as a better life or better job, and to clear one's path.

Candle Figure: Male or Female. Color black candles are used to make love die, to break up a relationship, or to do harm to another person.

In the old days when they used pins to prick their fingers and rub them together, saying "We're blood sisters." And the way back in time a woman would put blood in the man's coffee or food in order to keep him (because blood signifies a lasting bond), and some women have the man give her oral sex when she first began her period, so that he would suck the blood without even knowing it. Like drinking mother's milk, it's bonding. Does it really work? Should you try and find out? The answer to both is "Yes."

Spinster

Where everything is possible, growing up as a psychic and playing tricks on anyone who's there can be very interesting. I remember living in Salem, Massachusetts as a little girl. When I was seven, I went to sleep one day and felt like I went to hell and back. I went into a deep sleep and couldn't wake. My mother tried to get me up but couldn't for anything in the world. I desperately tried to get up, but couldn't. I felt as if there were bad spirits after my soul and also like there was so much knowledge to be gained. Finally, I woke up from my sleep. After a day and a half, as my hair and my clothes were soaking wet, I felt like I had traveled far away into another world, afraid I wouldn't come back to the one I knew.

There was this spinster-type old lady who lived next door and she grew very fond of me. She came over to my parents house and asked if I could go downtown Salem with her. My parents were a bit concerned about letting a complete stranger take me downtown. My mother said, "No." But my father said that it would be all right but not to stay long. He wanted to buy her car. It was a dark, green, four door Buick and sometimes I think that's the only reason he let me go.

We went downtown to a pizza parlor. I had a slice of Sicilian pizza and a sprite. I bought a book about witchcraft. I was curious. The old lady paid for it. We went back home and I went over to the old lady's place next door. It was a printing press. She lived in and owned it. I then made my very first diary of my life and bound it. I was so proud. She taught me how to read and write, encouraging and inspiring me greatly. She gave me this old type writer to use where I typed it on. I took it next door and before I could break the news, my sister took it and tore it to shreds. I was quite hurt. I was very fond of her and her of me, as well. She never married or had children but I know she loves me enough to try to buy me from my parents. She wanted for me to become very educated. She was very lonely; quite rich, too. And no one to leave it to or share it with. She mentioned it to my father and mother. They felt threatened. Then we moved away from there. She wanted me over at the printing shop all of the time. My parents felt threatened. She gave me a beautiful cat with blue eyes. I loved her and named her blue tiger.

The Witch

When I was a very young girl and living in Cambridge, Massachusetts, my sister and brother along with a neighborhood kid were walking. We saw an old lady through a window who was burning something in her front yard. She killed a white dove and buried it. She tried to light a match but couldn't. We leapt, hiding, and yelled, "You can't light a match. Ha, ha! Ha, ha!" yelling and laughing at her. One day we went back to her house and climbed over the gate and looked throughout the window into her kitchen. It was very dirty with lots of bottles everywhere. We saw a pigeon that she had killed and a white dove. She was trying to drain all of the blood out of it. It was horrifying. She turned quickly and came out of the door with a large butcher knife. We ran for our lives.

The Great Spook That Happens To Be Real

One day I went to Hermosa Beach, California. I met my first ghost. It was a man in the garage wearing old, dingy, dark grey clothes and a hat. My brother and I went into the garage together, and when we turned our heads we saw him. We jumped up and held one another. We looked at the old man and he made a mean face. We ran up to the house and said "Well, we're not going to tell anyone. They will think we're nuts. Okay, now promise not to tell anybody. Cross your heart and hope to die. No crossing your fingers or your toes."

When I was in the bathroom I felt something in there with me (this was before I went into the garage), and the presence was very strong and I felt as if it was a person, but I couldn't tell which sex it was. I knew it had died in that room of either a heart attack or a brain tumor- that the person had tried to get out for help but never made it. I felt like it wanted to hurt me. It was definitely evil- I knew that for sure. I was loosing my breath from fear and had to get out of there. I never mentioned it to anyone until my brother squealed to my other brother while trying to scare us, not knowing that there was really something in the house.

I remember when I was thirteen years old, I was in Philadelphia in front of a Catholic church that I would always walk my dog by. I felt safe there. I remember looking at the church lying down, eating a deviled dog and drinking a coke. I went into a phone booth and called home. The next thing I remember after that was waking up in the hospital at the University of Pennsylvania, the hospital I was born in. I was on the table, and, although my eyes were closed, I could see an open metal door with a handle on it. The door opened to the right and through the bright light I could see my mother, my uncle and a doctor. They had no idea I could see them, as far as they knew, I was dead. But I was fully aware of what they were saying. The doctor wanted to put me in the wall, telling my mother I was dead and that he would give her a death certificate. My uncle lied and said that I had taken my own life because that I was in love with his son.

I was furious with him. I could hear everything, and I was afraid of going into the wall. I said "I'm not dead now! Please don't put me in the wall!" but no one could hear me, and I couldn't move at all. I was in big trouble. The doctor told my mother that all my vital signs said I was dead, that the only thing I had going was a strong heart, but that he was sure that would be enough. She cried "But she's only thirteen years old!", and eventually convinced him to put me in intensive care.

From what I remember, I was in ICU for three days before my eyes finally opened. While I was there, my cat Blue Tiger walked over me and pulled me from my coma (I had cat scratches all over my chest when I awoke, and they hadn't been there when I arrived). The doctor was so shocked that he actually jumped when my eyes opened.

"Oh my God," he said. "Can you hear me? If you can, move your finger." I tried, but was too weak. "Move your little finger," he said. I was able to move that one up and down a very little bit. "Good. Blink your eyes if you can understand what I'm saying." I did, and he was convinced that I was going to be all right. He later told me: "You know, I was going to be all right. He later told me: "You know, I was going to put you in the wall. I thought you were dead."

I said, "I know. I heard everything; my uncle lying about me, the tag on my right toe, the metal door with the metal handle. I heard everything you said to my mother and everything else she said to you." He was shocked. I told him I saw everybody in a bright, white light. "Well, there was a bright light in the room," he said. "I know. It was a pure, white light. Very bright," I said. He asked me what had happened, and how the pills had gotten into my body. He said that there was a large amount of iron in my body and a lot of Tylenol. I told him I wasn't sure, but my mother told me the children were playing around and put them in my drink.

My sister waited for the doctor to leave before she came and smacked me. "You scared me to death," she said. "Do you know what kind of trouble you've gotten us into? The social workers are coming to investigate us!" She told me to stick the story my mother told, or they might take me away.

People come to a psychic for many different reasons. Some for entertainment purposes, some or answers to their questions, some looking for the right decisions. Others come looking to remove evil spirits, others are psychics themselves looking to develop their craft. Some can only read cards, or palms, or both. Some only make the oil (which is really hard, if you ask me), and others to mix herbs. Some people come to psychics to be successful in business. Some cases are different, such as past-life karma that can get in the way unless you regress it. To even the past and go into the future is very important!

First of all, you have to find a psychic who is genuine and very experienced in what she does, and then follow the work with all your belief. When you talk about your magic to others you weaken it! In other words, you shouldn't add doubt to your work or tell others , because it is sacred to you.

However, you also get these wannabes, psychics who are not blood born and have an obsession for power that they long for. Use your judgment. And of course, you never want to get any psychic really mad at you, because you never know what they will cast upon you (Of course, depending on the day and time, it could come back on them).

My uncle once said, "If you can't say anything nice, then don't say anything at all." Not a bad thing to practice. There are some psychics that give the rest bad names because they are phonies. But what they don't understand is that they are dealing with the supernatural. So even if a psychic is not a real believer in what she does, the bargain she made with the client is already established in the supernatural world. But in some cases, a client's belief is so strong that it works because it's a thought made with a strong belief that overpowers the negative. The spirits know the client's wish, and will grant it to him/her.

The Chinese believe that the psychic doesn't remove the bad spirits because it is too dangerous, which may be true. It's their belief that you can confuse the spirits and make them go away for awhile, perhaps for a few years or so. But they can be removed forever. Take the Winchester House, for example. By constantly building and adding more rooms, you trap and confuse the spirits.

You can also use sage, myrrh and frankincense to suppress the spirits. These are also great for cleansing past lives as well as the present.

The Cat Candles

1. Take two red, pillared candles. Carve a cat's head into each one, complete with eyes, whiskers, mouth, nose and ears (carve it deep). Write the appropriate names on it, with the female name on the female cat and the male name on the male cat. Now that we have that straight, put out a sheet of virgin parchment paper. Draw a big heart on the paper and date it. In dragon blood ink, write your name on one side of the heart, and your love's name on the other side. Now write your intention in the middle. Then put honey all over the candle, and sprinkle some cinnamon on top, as well as some dragon blood powder around the side. Now face the candles towards one another and light them. You can burn them for one to two hours a day, or longer if you have the time. Remember to snuff them out when you're finished. No one can touch these candles, for they are dedicated to love.

One love potion involves a bunch of pink and red carnations and a bottle of wine and fusing them together. That's a love potion. For example, take one dozen flowers and a bottle of wine or champagne, mix them together, and let them sit in a refrigerator for a few hours. Then take out the flowers, pour your magic into a bottle, and serve it to the one you love. Place a red ribbon around the bottle for it represents the red cord.

The Hair Ritual

2. Another love ritual involves taking a piece of the hair and a piece of your hair, tying them together in the center. Make one knot, then another twelve knots. Focus on what you want to come out of the relationship. Put some neroli oil on the hair and voodoo night love potion on the wrist, and, both sides of the neck. You can sew yourself a mojo bag with red cotton material or red velvet material. You sew two sides of the bag with red thread in a circular motion, very tightly stitched. Then, place the hair into the bag and tie it with a red rope, red ribbon or a red shoe string. You must wear it until your partner commits to you. Then hide it and never let it come undone. If you let it come undone, so will the relationship. A safe deposit box would be a good place to hide it after you get your commitment. Then hide it and never let it come undone or your relationship will then become undone. External use only.

1. Another love potion is to cook with garlic. It purifies the body and works as a protective to keep you strong, as well as to bring together families. Rosemary works well, too.

2. Or, take a red candle and write the person's name on it seven times. Anoint it with red rose oil. Place a picture of the person and a red rose (for the power of Rosa) and place them by the candle. Place these on a table and project your thoughts of what you want, whether you want them to come over or call you. Use your willpower, and be positive.

3. There is also dream magic. You can take something of theirs and place it in your bedroom by your stuff. Go to sleep and pull him with your thoughts. Some people are stronger in their dreams, so this may work better.

4. You can also write your command on a piece of parchment paper in red or dragon blood ink. Focus on what you are doing, and burn it in the fire place, or in the woods (which would be better because you are closer to nature). Sit in the Indian position and focus while you do this. Nothing else should exist this moment, only what you see and what is real.

5. Mixing lavender and rosebuds together will make you feel more beautiful and feminine.

6. Take two pictures of two people are fighting and a red and black reversible candle. Carve their names in the candle and what it is you want to reverse between them. Snuff out the candle (never blow it out or you'll undo the magic). Do not wish harm; remember, you're working with a reversible candle.

The Mirror Box

Now the mirror boxes. Place the name of the person in the box. You see, it sends their karma back to them, and they have to get their karma right before the earth will leave them alone. It sends their energy back to them, and if the person is bad they'll have a lot to deal with. They cannot get out of the box unless they break it or dig it up, which would be next to impossible if they can't dig it up (so don't tell anyone where you buried it). Like it so far? Well, this is what you do:

Step 1: Use a cigar box or a candy box. Glue a mirror on the top of the box, and another on the bottom.

Step 2: Write the person's name on the parchment paper in big block letters, and then cut them out. If you have a picture of the person, you can glue it to the bottom mirror and it will reflect their karma back to them.

Step 3: You need to take a dark blue candle- or, if they hurt you badly, a black one- use the hot wax to seal the box. Now you're ready for:

Step 4: Sew a bag from purple cloth (preferably cotton) and purple thread, in a circular fashion. Make sure the stitches are tight. Slip the box inside and tightly tie the bag shut with purple ribbon.

Step 5: Dig a hole into the ground, preferably in the woods where it would be tough to find. Put the box in, and pour mandrake oil into the open hole and command that this person receive all the karma from the earth and the four corners of the universe. Lift up your hands and say: "I command the four corners of the universe to hear my plea and enter in this ceremony today (or tonite, whichever is appropriate)." Now drop the empty bottle in the ground. Tell the universe what this person has done and how you feel. Now fill the hole and walk away. Leave it there forever. The box will stop automatically when the person has learned their lesson, which means you can't hurt people and say it's okay, because karma will get you, too. Good luck with this ritual.

Page 15

1. A yellow candle is for change. Take pieces of parchment paper and write on it what you want to change in your life in dove blood ink or dragon blood ink.

2. A blue candle is for healing, or for spiritual guidance. If you are using it for healing, write your name or the name of the person you want to heal on it seven times, and then put healing oil on it. Focus your mind on your magical goal of healing. Visualize yourself or your sick friend clearly in your mind. Do not see sickness, visualize only perfect health. If the sickness enters your mind, banish it immediately; it will only hinder the magic. Open the oil while concentrating and put the oil on you with your right hand (for everything to go right). Hold the candle with your left hand (or use a candle holder) to put the oil on it until it is covered with healing oil. Now you can pray to God to help him or her. Circle the person with your mind in white healing energy from head to toe. Then put blue healing light around that. Now ask for sins they have committed- or that that you have committed, if you are related- to be forgiven. Plead to God, cry if necessary and ask for forgiveness. Repent with all your might.

If you have the person there, put the white sage around the person in a circle. Take a small frying pan with some frankincense and myrrh and light it with matches. Also, amber is a good stone for healing, as are Amethyst, tiger's eye, hematite, Botswana agate, clear crystal, and turquoise. Give the person some lavender to bathe in, and place a red ribbon on the person for protection from evil.

You can do this ritual outside on the grass with the person when the son is shining. Then take them out of the circle and don't let them re-enter it. Throw away the sage when you're done. You can also buy their illness, but the mother and father have to sell it. Try a silver dollar or silver quarter. Take it, and then banish it out of you. My uncle did this once (that I know of).

3. A purple candle is the master candle. Write your name on it. Now you are the master of the situation.

4. A white candle is for purity.

5. A forest-green candle is for money. Use the one that is all natural with no scent. A good place to find these is at a Walgreen's drugstore. Just light and say "money".

6. A red candle is for love, especially if you put a red rose next to it.

Page 17

7. A pink candle is for friendship, or to keep a lover faithful. Take a seashell and place it in the center of the room. Use salt to make a circle around it. Step inside the circle with two pink candles and some water from your sink (or some well water). Say to the goddess Dorka: "Keep my loved one faithful to me." Carve your name into one candle and his into the other. Cha moonda witch *a* A clap your hands three times. Repeat 3 times, 3 times in a row.

8. Gray candles and black-and-white candles are uncrossing candles. You can get these in New Orleans, Los Angeles, or Lower Manhattan. They are to uncross you. I've never used one-I uncross the old-fashioned way.

9. An orange candle is used for encouragement, and it strengthens the ability to concentrate and stimulate.

10. A brown candle represents uncertainty, doubt, neutrality and hesitation.

Sin Eating

Step 1. Sin eating usually takes place at a wake. You eat the deceased's sins so that they can go to heaven. It's not good to eat at a funeral parlor, though. I would take my family home or to a restaurant to eat.

Cemetery

Step 1: When you leave a cemetery, you should pick a branch from a tree and throw it out as you leave the cemetery gate. You should also never point at a cemetery; it's bad luck.

So the spirit will remain in the cemetery; also it is a good idea to stop somewhere after leaving the cemetery and buy something before going home, just to make sure you didn't take a ghost home with you.

Step 2: If you are mourning someone who was close to you, you're stuck in the clothing you have on at that time for three days because the dead walk the earth for three days to say good-bye. Since you've been stuck in those clothes for such a long time, you should throw them out afterwards, no matter how expensive they were. You must also take off all jewelry, and you must wear no makeup at all for at least three days. The spouse of the deceased should mourn six months to a year to show proper respect.

Every time that you mention the dead by name you wake them. So when you do mention their name, say "May thy rest in peace, day nam my ja nas doud a menda."

You can also honor the dead by feeding them. You can go to the grave and pour water on their grave for them to drink, and even light them a cigarette and lay some food by their graveside. Or, you can set up in your home a special room where you can feed them their favorite food. Saturday is the day of the dead, but you can feed them any day you wish in small amounts. In your mind you will see some of the food gone, or a bite taken out. Don't be alarmed, they are accepting your offering.

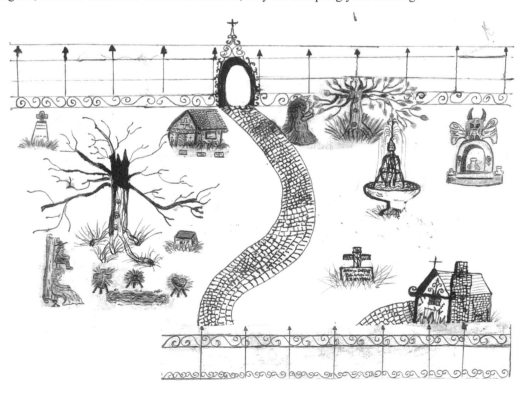

Healing oil is used for healing, of course.

Heliotripe is used with incense and candles to gain power over someone. You can also wear it to gain power over someone.

High John the Conqueror oil, candle, wood, and powder all in one candle is very powerful. Use it to gain money, strength, and success, but you have to project it.

Ylang ylang candles are being made by many candle makers and are becoming very popular because they promote peace and tranquility. You can also use them to do peace rituals.

If you put some almond or coconuts in a person's pocket it brings them closer to you.

To control others, wear bend-over oil on your hands or use some to anoint a candle. It bends one's will to your commands.

Drawing oil will bring back a straying lover. Sprinkle some on their clothes, or put some on a pink candle and let it burn for seven days.

Frankincense is one of the strongest oils of all. It comes in rock or oil form. Use it to anoint an alter. This is used in Catholic churches and also in funeral homes to sedate spirits.

Amber is also used for healing, and it comes as stone or as oil.

Gardenia flower is used for peace, love and spirituality. It comes in oil or perfume form.

Lavender brings peace and comfort. Most brides bathe in lavender before the wedding ceremony. Also, lavender chimes work to fight off evil spirits.

Controlling oil or powder is used to control the will of others.

Mandrake is easy to get in Texas (it seems like it grows all over the place). It is also known as Satan's apple, and you can put it on your red candle during the day for love or at night for hexing.

Musk has been known for years as a very soothing love potion that brings nature closer together.

Bathe in orris root draw love from the opposite sex.

Patchouli arouses the passions of both sexes.

If you can get honeysuckle from a tree, put some on a red candle- it's great for love rituals.

Drink bright-eye bolk like a tea to heighten your awareness.

Kitchen Stock

1. Get some fresh garlic, myrrh and frankincense.
2. Some white, red, green and blue candles. They should be all-natural with a virgin wick.
3. Also: Pink candles, a yellow candle, a purple candle and both a white and red skull candle.
4. Some cinnamon, a jar of honey and parsley.
5. Some basil- fresh or dry- red wine and champagne.
6. Some basil seeds in a packet, some roses and pansy flowers in the yard.
7. Some virgin parchment paper, two rolls of rope or ribbon- one red and one purple- and some velvet material.
8. A package of needles, as well as some purple cotton material.
9. A bottle of dragon blood, a bottle of dove blood and a red ink pen.
10. Red and purple thread.
11. A cigar box or candy box, some uncrossing oil and some peace oil.
12. Some master oil, rose oil (red and white), some controlling powder, jinx removing powder and two reversible candles (one red-and-black, one green-and-black).
13. Two red figures, one male and one female.
14. Some seashells and a bottle of springwater.
15. Seven African Powers spiritual incense.
16. Peaceful home spiritual incense.
17. Van van incense.
18. Break-up powder
19. Uncrossing powder for protection from enemies.
20. Some black water to fight enemies.
21. White sage leaf.
22. Some High John the Conqueror oil, wood and powder.
23. Some mandrake oil.

24. Bulk lavender.

25. Dried rose buds.

26. Some lucky hand root.

27. Golden Seal powder.

28. Hyssop.

29. Nutmeg.

30. Mistletoe.

31. Valerian root.

32. Bulk verbena.

33. Bulk witch hazel.

34. Some oak leaves-preferably a big garbage bag full- and an acorn.

35. Wormwood.

36. White oak bark.

37. Sea salt.

38. Skull cap.

39. Burdock root.

40. Comfrey.

41. Oak bark.

42. Yarrow.

43. Yellow dock.

44. Slippery elm.

Stone

Also:

1. Amethyst- Used for healing

2. Hematite- Used for grounding to the universe and for protection

3. Lapis- Used for spiritual heightening

4. Rose quartz - used for friendship or to attract love and serenity

5. Tiger's Eye- Strictly for luck

6. Turquoise- When given, it will result in pregnancy

7. Camellia- Old stone used for guiding and healing

8. Crystals- For clearing negativity

9. Malachite- Used for obtaining money and luck

A frying pan (for magic only)

Vegetable oil

Some Hot Foot oil- When placed on the door knob of a house or car handle, the individual touching it will never want to return. It has been used to make people leave a job or move.

Some Evitis oil (at my client's request I cannot release the formula for breaking up people- it can be very destructive and can be very dangerous in the wrong hands. Sorry- maybe in the next life).

Waxing moon, New (Full) Moon, Waning Moon, New (Full) Moon

1. Midnight for banishing.
2. Sunset for finding the truth.
3. Midday for extra power.
4. Sunrise for a new start.
5. Waxing moon for growth.
6. Waning moon for letting go of things.
7. Black moon- no magic is recommended
8. East winds for intellectual change.
9. South wind is very passionate for lovers.
10. North wind is for separation
11. West wind is for cleansing and soothing one's soul.

Chakra Balancing

Red: Love passion, energy, enthusiasm, courage- first chakra

Orange: Strength, authority, attraction, joy, success- second chakra.

Yellow: Clairvoyance, learning, mind, communication,- third chakra.

Green: Healing, money, prosperity, luck, fertility- fourth chakra.

Blue: Healing,, mediation, tranquillity, forgiveness- fifth chakra

Lavender: Intuition, dignity, spiritual shield- sixth chakra.

White: Protection, peace, purity, truth- seventh chakra.

Pink: Emotional love, friendship, affection, harmony- fourth chakra.

Turquoise: Awareness, meditation, moon, creativity- fifth chakra

Sea Green: Emotional, healing, protection and calming- fourth chakra.

Rose: Self-love, enhancement, of relationships- fourth chakra.

Black: Absorption, destruction of negative energy- first chakra.

Peach: Gentle strength, joy- second chakra.

Purple: Spirituality, wisdom, psychic awareness- sixth and seventh chakra.

Silver-blue: Deep wisdom, intuition, the moon- sixth chakra

Gold: The sun, financial matters, prosperity- Yang

Silver: The moon, female energy- Yin.

Planets

1. Sunday is ruled by the moon. The color is yellow, which means change, honor, glory, socializing, peace and harmony.

2. Monday is ruled by the moon. It's color is white- reconciliation, voyages, message of female fertility.

3. Tuesday is ruled by Mars. It's color is red- defying of enemies, breaking negative spells, development of positive energy. It can also be for negative purpose.

4. Wednesday is ruled by mercury. It's color is purple- psychic and spiritual communications, divination and influencing others.

5. Thursday is ruled by Jupiter. It's color is blue- male fertility, health, luck, success, honors wealth. Begin your rituals.

6. Friday is ruled by Venus. It's color is green- love, romance, beauty, gratification, of lust, friendships, (party night!).

7. Saturday is ruled by Saturn. It's color is black- protection from evil, spirit communications, anything connected to the home.

The Body Is Just An Instrument

Your body is just an instrument. Your soul and your mind is everything. Sometimes people are attracted to the outside, only to find that the inside stinks. Never judge a book by its cover, because when the passion dies or wears off, you still have to live with and build a future with the person you're married to.

So listen to Lana. Before you destroy yourself, ask yourself: "What makes me happy?" And what do I need from another human being? Is it money? Is it consideration? Respect? Sex? Companionship? What do we have in common besides attraction for one another? Would he be a good father? Would she be a good mother?

It's very important to know the family background, such as mental illnesses or diseases you may inherit. Also pay attention to what kind of father and mother he/she has, because that can create a lot of negativity for you. If the father cheated, it will go on for three generations. Marriage is very serious.

If your mind is still made up after that long Mother Hubbard talk, then let's continue. Your body is just an instrument. Your mind and soul are everything. With your soul, you can will people to feel the energy of your thoughts. That's why God and Satan let you make your own decisions. Your mind is the key to magic. If you can see it and believe it, then it exists in your world. Do not ever allow doubt into your world- it's negative. Think positive. Remember the power of positive thinking. First it becomes a thought, then it becomes doing, then it becomes reality.

Make a list of the ten most important things in your life. Write them on a piece of paper and place it on your wall (tape it up there, if you have to). Go to it everyday. It will become a thought, then an action, then reality. See yourself doing what you want. Visualize it. Hold it. Push it. The next thing you know, it will happen. Voila

Miracles

Most people come to me for help and it is so gratifying when they receive their wishes. I can't explain how happy and proud I am to see a happy ending.

For example- a guy broke up with his girlfriend and I got her back for him. But he's not ready to take the next big step until he finishes school. Which is probably the right thing to do. He needs to grow up as a man and become more financially stable for his self esteem. A woman came to me wanting help with her love life but did not want to pay my fee. So how could I help her when she put the issue of money between us? Just because I am Lana, people don't give me my supplies for free. She had spent money on other psychics, very little from what I gathered, so the moral is that there are no cheap ways out. You must put in the money and the time. What you put in is what you get out of it. Eventually, she left her husband and also left the country. Guess what? Her husband came to me with her picture and asked me to read her. I was shocked when I saw the photo being her and did not reveal to him the fact that I had consulted with her. That would be overstepping the bounds of privacy. But, I explained what her problem was, still trying to help them. But he didn't want to pay, either. So, perhaps he got the results he deserved.

One thing I've learned is that you pay for it, one way or another. If someone can show you the way to solve your problem with their knowledge and expertise while saving you much grief in love, then why not?

Also, sometimes, a client walks in and says ok....I want it to work. But, sometimes, I can see that their soul is not really in it. They want a straight out buy without the faith. It is not a good situation. They already have lost because they doubt that magic exists. And, they want to buy it. Magic is very special. It doesn't like people who doubt it. But it may not work if their doubt is too strong. For example, you cannot go into the church and say, "Oh, god, if you're really there....please help me." And then later say, "You didn't help me, so you're not real." God knows who believes with their heart and who is faking. And that's why some people receive miracles and others don't. You must have patience in everything you do, whether it is magic or prayer. God is magic. He can move mountains if he wants to. He can heal you in the split of a second if he chooses you.

Let me tell you a story. I was in a horrible car accident one night while I found myself bleeding from the mouth. I couldn't walk and took many painkillers but the pain wouldn't stop. One day, I looked up at the sky through my bedroom window, and with tears in my eyes, and said, "God, who did I hurt in my life? What have I done wrong? If I have done something to somebody, I am sorry. Please forgive me, for I didn't mean to hurt anyone whether they hurt me first or not. Then, the pain stopped all of a sudden. I also stopped bleeding from the mouth. I got out of the bed on my own for the first time in months and reached up into the air with my hands and bent down, touching my toes with no pain at all. I jumped up and did jumping jacks. I ran all over my condo laughing. It was a miracle. I went to my doctor in Beverly Hills and he told me that I shouldn't stand by myself and that I would fall. The nurse came to help me but I laughed. Look, I said, I can walk on my own. They were in shock. I bent Down and ran around the office. The nurse cried that it was a miracle. The doctor said, "I can't explain it." And the nurse kissed her rosemary and said, "I can. God helped her." She kneeled when she did this. The doctor didn't believe in miracles. But I said, yes, God helped me. I had spoken to him the night before and had repented of all my sins. Look at me. No more blood. Cancel the back surgery, doctor, for God hath saved me. He seemed confused but could not explain how I was walking, when for months I wasn't even able to stand or walk. The doctor said, "Well, I don't believe in God, but something happened here. You're well, so maybe there is a god after all. We'll have to say that it's a miracle because there is no other explanation for how you can do what you're doing." The office was so happy that they laughed, kissed me and said good luck. The nurse said, "I knew there was a God. I always knew it." She then kissed her rosemary and made a sign of the cross.

And while we're talking about miracles, there is a Church called Saint Anne de Beaupre in Quebec that is known for it's miracles. When I was a little girl, about six or seven, my father had gone to Boston General Hospital with a broken leg. The doctors took an x-ray of his leg and said that it had an infection and would have too come off. My father yelled, "Oh, no you don't. Get way from me, but..."

The Powers Of God, Mother Mary And Saint Ann Work In Mysterious Ways

"You have to," the doctor said. My father cried and said, "I'm going to see Mother Mary," drove to Canada to the Church, Saint Ann de Beaupre. There were one hundred steps he had to climb on crutches. My mother and I were so scared because if he fell, he would have died. He reached the top of the church and went to Mother Mary. There were crutches hanging from the ceiling and all around us were wheelchairs, braces and eyeglasses by those who had been healed. My father was talking to Mother Mary. And she glowed as if she came to life. I could see a white light and a blue light surrounding them. There was a sound that was hard to describe. I could tell you that they were talking but couldn't tell about what. I couldn't hear their conversation. She shed a tear and then my father dropped his crutches and walked. Everyone in the church turned and looked at my father. They put money in the top of his cast as he danced down the steps. He went back to the doctor and said, "Cut off this cast please." He did this as he smiled from ear to ear. They said, "Oh, know. We have to amputate your leg." He said, "Oh, know. I'm healed. I don't need the cast anymore." He convinced the doctor to take a new x-ray of his leg. When the doctor saw the x-ray of his leg, the doctor was confused. "This is not the same," said the doctor. "Why, you're leg has no infection and was never broken. There must be some mistake." He was shocked. "We better get you out of this cast right now," he said. "I'm so sorry. We must have had someone else's x-ray. I don't know why they put this on you. I apologize." My father said, "You poor thing. That x-ray was mine, but I had a talk with Mother Mary and she healed me." The doctor didn't know what to say, they never do when it comes to miracles. So you see, miracles do exist.

Once, when I was pregnant with my first daughter and living in San Francisco, the doctor said my bag had torn and only one of us could live. He asked me to sign a paper saying who I would choose. I chose my daughter's life. "Are you sure?" he asked. "You can always have another baby." I said, "No, let her live," and I signed the form.

The funny thing was some wonderful old lady whom I didn't even know took me to the hospital. She put me in under her daughter's name for insurance purposes so that the hospital wouldn't kick me out. She knew I was sick and she knew who I was and who my family was, but I had never met her. She cried

Picture of God taken at St. Anne de Beaupre's Church in old Quebec

(Look In Center of Page)

and said that she was trying to find my mother and sister. We got my mother and my sister on the phone and they were very ungrateful to her. I started bleeding in a coffee shop and she and her family rushed me to the hospital. Well lo and behold, my mother and my sister moved me from that hospital to another one. somewhere in the bay area. My sister had other plans for me. She smacked me in the face and said, "You can't keep the baby. You're going to live but the baby won't make it." I won't let you die." The doctor took a look at me and said the bag had mended itself. My sister had wanted her doctor friend to give me a cut-and-tie so that I could never bear children again, and he was willing to do it behind my back before my bag had mended. The nurses at the other hospital had seen that, and so there were witnesses. They took me out of the hospital by ambulance to the second hospital. When I arrived at the second hospital, the nurse came in and changed the sheets for the bleeding and looked at the vagina. She blotted with some sort of cloth and cleansed the area. She noticed the blood starting to clot, so she had the doctor look at it. The doctor looked and the bag, by then, had mended itself. She argued with her doctor friend on the side to get rid of the baby, but the doctor was not willing to loose his license over murder. The doctor further explained that, because of the healing which had occurred, the child bearing would take place. Furthermore, the doctor wanted to keep me in the hospital for loss of blood and to slow the contractions which were occurring, but agreed to release me to return home for bed rest. When, in October, when I was to deliver in LA at Cedars Sinai, the nurses gave me too much anesthesia to stop the contractions. They said to stop screaming and that I was scaring the other patients. I explained that it hurt so much. A little short nurse told me, "Oh, come on...It doesn't hurt that bad. You're more frightened than anything; it's your first baby." She patted me lightly on top of my head. I said, "I'm sorry. I don't mean to scream. It's just that it hurts so bad. Where's my doctor? It's been over an hour, at least." She explained that he would come shortly. So I asked the nurse, "How many children did you have?" She replied, "Oh, I've never had any. " So, I told her to very curtly to please shut the fuck up. The other patients began yelling in hysterics that they, too, had been waiting for the doctor to arrive for hours. Finally, my little gay doctor arrived. I had figured that he had enough sex, now he was on duty.....time to be a doctor. He soon learned that she had been sedated beyond reason; certainly beyond the opportunity to bear a child. Another doctor within the delivery ward tried to induce labor.

Magical Plants and Flowers

Tulips are always good for mending break-ups and repairing relationships. I prefer red or white tulips for peace and tranquillity. It works best if you also use a candle that matches your desires. Put the flower on a coffee table with the candle and the right shade of table cloth.

Chinese orchids are good, too. They bring money and harmony into the home.

A money tree is also lucky, and the jade plant will also draw money into a business or home. Place it on a pedestal with a red flower on the left side and a yellow flower on the right side beneath it.

The San Jose plant is a lucky plant as well. It brings money and happiness. Juniper does, too (I have one, personally). It comes in blue and green and both are gorgeous.

There is also the Witch's plant (Jereo plant in Spanish). Put money- quarters, nickels or dimes but no pennies (it doesn't like pennies)- in it with some water to sink into. You must leave the money in there. You can purchase one at a botanical. Just put it in a large soup bowl half-full of water with your money and you're done.

Hollywood's Ghost Story

This is a true story. My cousin rented an apartment in Hollywood and moved upstairs. The previous occupant, a woman, had been murdered in it. Apparently, there had been a break in and the woman had been killed. She had been cremated and her ashes were put in an urn and left on top of the fireplace. My cousin had moved in right after her divorce and was recovering from a broken leg. She started to clean the apartment and by mistake dumped the ashes out of the urn into the sink. By doing so, she had trapped the murdered woman in the house now and forever. The woman appeared to my cousin and said "Get out of my house!" My cousin said "No. I have no place to go. I'm not leaving; you go." She was very bitter from her divorces, and the other lady was bitter, too- especially after losing her life. My cousin told the ghost to shut up and be quiet, or she would get rid of her. The dead lady got so mad she beat the shit out of my cousin. She said to my cousin, "Get out of my house! I want you out of my house!", and threw her down the stairs. Sure enough, my cousin called the landlord and said "You have a ghost in here. I need back the money I gave you sir. Please."

"oh, no," said the landlord. "You're breaking the lease."

"Sir, I got the shit knocked out of me by your ghost," my cousin said. "You didn't tell me you have a dead person in here."

The landlord said, "I suppose I should have told you, but everybody moves out when I do and I needed to rent the place. She bothers everybody that I rent to. I'm going to lose my investment. She was beaten and raped and thrown down the stairs by some guys who stole some of her jewelry."

"I see," said my cousin. "Now I understand. Never mind sir. I'll call you back."

She tried to reason with the ghost, but it wouldn't stop crying and saying, "I am stuck in this house forever. My life was taken away. You're alive. Get out of my house. Leave me alone or I will kill you."

"I'm sorry for what happened to you," my cousin said. "All right. I'll leave you alone to find peace.

"I'm sorry for what happened to you. You're right, it wasn't fair." Then they brought in a priest and he freed her soul from the house. What had been done to her was too shocking for her to get over."

About Past-Life Regression And Time Travel

When you don't get it right, you will come back again. That's why we do past-life regressions. It tells us who we were and what kind of lives we had, what kind of karma we have and what needs to be corrected. You must get it right or you'll repeat it. And that's what past life regression is all about. It gives you a lot of information. For example, take deja vu. That's not you're brain rewinding in the middle of the street, that's time hitting you, meaning you either did this before or it was meant to happen and you weren't paying attention (to your dreams, most likely). You could also have known someone from a past life and end up meeting them in this life as well. If you messed them up in a past life and you meet them in this one, you should try to make it better. It's for your own good and I strongly suggest it. You've got to get it right or it will keep coming back again and again, and you don't want that. Or do you?

The Self Conscious Mind and Putting Your Priorities In Perspective

I can tell what people want when they walk into my office by the colors they wear. The subconscious mind dresses them in what they want, and the conscious mind is not even aware most of the time. People can be their own best friend or their own worst enemy.

Again, my method is that it becomes a thought, then it becomes doing and then it becomes reality.

You should make a list of the ten most important things in your life on a piece of paper and hang it where you will see it all of the time. Then look at it everyday. Remember, it becomes a thought, then doing, then reality. When you succeed, make a star. When you have a hard time, do it over again until it becomes reality. If you allow negativity, you will receive negative results. If you stay positive, then you'll receive positive results. Good luck to you.

Oh, by the way, words are older than magic. And what you say holds a lot of power. For example, good luck. I wish you well. Have a nice day. Or, God forbid, when someone dies....rest in peace. Or, for better or for worse. For richer, for poorer. In sickness and in health. Until death do you part. That's one of my favorites. When a minister performs a ritual, it is for a reason. When he blesses one's soul or body, it is for a purpose. When he blesses an alter, it's for another reason. So, you see, words are power and always will be. They can be a blessing or they can do harm. So think before you say or do. You can run but not hide. Karma will find you everywhere.

In the old days, they would cast out negative energy by putting it into a stone or some personal jewelry. And throwing it into a river or a pond. You can do the same, remember. Night time is always recommended for banishing. Also, you can use a watch to bring two people together in time or to separate them, depending on how you see it. It must be sacrificed as part of the ritual. Another way of giving to the earth is through mother nature. In Africa, they bury gold so as to walk on gold and have the earth bear them riches. Some burial stones, so as not to wither as a leaf in the wind.

The Chinese Zodiac

Rabbit (1915, 27, 39, 51, 63, 75, 87, 99)- You are the kind of person with whom people like to be around: affectionate, obliging, always pleasant. You have a tendency, though, to get sentimental and superficial.

Dragon (1916, 28, 40, 52, 64, 76, 88, 2000)- Full of vitality and enthusiasm, the dragon is a popular individual, even though he or she has the reputation of being foolhardy and having a "big mouth" at times. You are intelligent, gifted, and a perfectionist.

Snake (1917, 29, 41, 53, 65, 77, 89, 2001)- Rich in wisdom and charm, you are romantic and deep thinking and your intuition guides. Avoid procrastination, and your stingy attitude towards money and keep your sense of humor.

Horse (1918, 30, 42, 54, 66, 78, 90, 2002)- Your capacity for work is amazing. You are your own person, very intelligent, and friendly. You have a strong selfish streak and is very sharp and cunning.

Goat (1919, 31, 43, 55, 67, 79, 91, 2003)- You're charming company, even though you're always starting off on the wrong foot. Sheep are intelligent and artistic, but always the first to complain.

Monkey (1920, 32, 44, 56, 68, 80, 92, 2004)- Monkeys are smart and clever wit. You have a strong nature and magnetic personality. Avoid being opportunistic and distrustful of others.

Cock (1921, 33, 45, 57, 69, 81, 93, 2005)- The cock is a hard worker, shrewd and definite in decision making, and often speaks his or her mind.

Dog (1922, 34, 46, 58, 70, 82, 94, 2006)- The dog will never let you down. You are honest and faithful to those you love. You are plagued by constant worry, a sharp tongue and a tendency to find fault.

Boar (1923, 35, 47, 59, 71, 83, 95, 2007)- You're a splendid companion, an intellectual with a very strong need to set difficult goals. You are sincere, tolerant, and honest, but- by expecting the same of others- you are naive.

Rat (1924, 36, 48, 60, 72, 84, 96, 2008)- You are imaginative, charming, and truly generous to the person you love. However, you have a quick tendency to be quick-tempered and overly critical. You are also inclined towards being an opportunist.

Ox (1925, 37, 49, 61, 73, 85, 97, 2009)- You are a born leader, inspiring confidence from all others. Oxen are conservative, formal and good with their hands. Avoid being chauvinistic and demanding.

Tiger (1926, 38, 50, 62, 74, 86, 2010)- Tigers are sensitive, emotional and possess great love. However, you get carried away, are willful of what you think is right and rebellious.

The Treasure of May Dew

On the morning of May, place a gold dish on your front door and leave it overnight. The next morning, place it on your lips and rub it on your face while saying your lover's name. Toss it over your shoulder. You will see your love grow strong and be very happy together.

You can make a potion of this with May flowers. Use pansies, either red roses or pure rose oil, a vanilla pod and some red wine. You will then have a demonstrative you never imagined could exist.

If you want to attract love, then wear peach, green, yellow, white, purple, lavender or soft pink, especially if you have clothes in which colors are mixed. Wear soft clothes, such as Egyptian cotton, silk, or light rayon.

Gardens Are Very Enchanting

While bringing peace and harmony, especially with a waterfall. You should plant some gardenias, pansies and roses. Rose briars are wonderful. As are tulips, jade plants and money trees. You should also have red, white and pink carnations. And lots of charms to keep bad spirits away. Fish ponds are also very lucky.

Wishbone

When you get a wishbone from a turkey or chicken, you should close your eyes and make a wish. Who ever gets their wish on Friday, wish for love; on Monday, wish for a new beginning and peace and harmony.

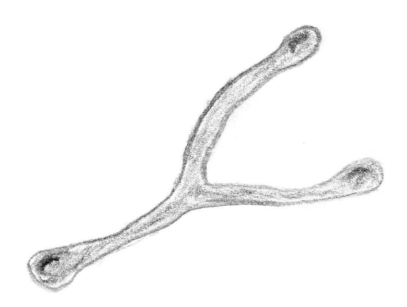

We later moved into a new place in Connecticut. It was very cold. I remember looking out the window and it was snowing. My sister backed out the driveway and ran over my cat, crushing its head. I was told Blue Tiger was dead. Later I was told by my other sister that she let the cat out of the house on purpose. I felt it was time to get even with her for what she had done-- first my diary and then my cat. Her day was to come.

I pulled out my book on magic and did a spell on her. It was my first spell. I took a red pen and wrote on a piece of paper what I wanted to happen to her and placed it with a lemon under a steam furnace. My other sister found the book under my pillow and said: "What are you doing with this book? It's evil. What have you done? Tell me!" Then they started looking around the house and outside in the yard and by the car. They found it and pulled it apart and buried it. She said: "You mustn't do things like that, for they will come back at you."

That's when it all began. Later I found out that half of my cousins and aunts were practicing witchcraft.-- white and black magic on one another. They wish bad things and good things on another, depending on if they're mad or not. We were all scared of my uncle because everything he said, would happen. We knew he was powerful. My cousin was in the kitchen one day and she told me my grandmother's maiden name was Uwanawitch, as well. That explained a lot of things.

Superstition

1. Never let a pole pass between you when you're walking with someone, it will split you apart.

2. Never walk through a rainbow; they're sacred to God and it's bad luck to do so.

3. It's back luck to point at the cemetery. If you do so, bite your finger just a little bit to be forgiven.

4. It is both bad luck and disrespect to the dead to walk on a grave.

5. Never leave a cemetery without cutting a branch of a tree and throwing it out as you leave. You can take it with you when you go, but you don't want to do that.

6. Never put your feet on the table, it's bad luck.

7. Never say and mean, "May the devil take my soul," he just might. He always listens and waits for that special moment when you're weak. Beware.

8. Always wash your face before you face the world in the morning. It's good luck.

9. Never covet someone else's wife or husband, because it will come to you.

10. Don't make fun of the handicapped, God will smite you for doing so.

11. Don't badmouth the wind or the sun, they can hurt you.

The Itchy Hand

When your hand itches, kiss it quick and rub it on your hair. The right hand means money is coming your way. When the left hand itches it's not so good. It means your going to spend money.

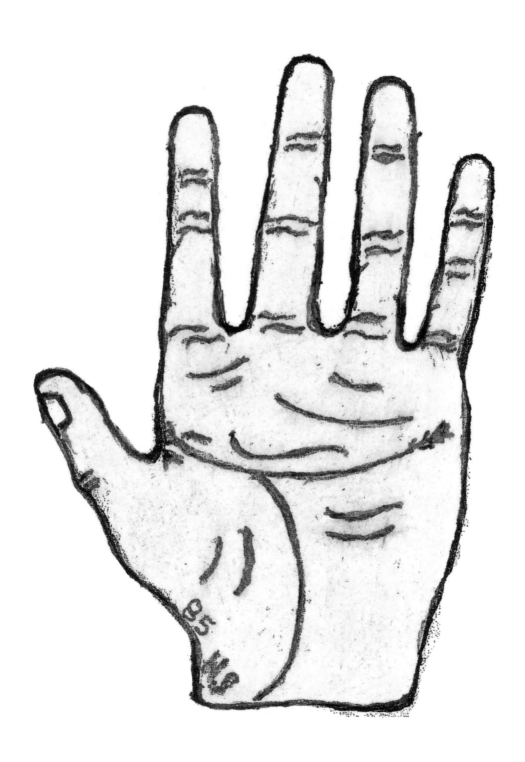

The Eyes

When the right eye twitches, something bad is about to happen. When the left eye twitches, it's good luck. Some people say that when some people put the evil eye on you, then one or both eyes will twitch. My advice is to stay home until this passes.

Psalm 70

When trying to get someone's face off of you, then read Psalm 70, the Psalm of David to the chief musician, to bring remembrance:

"Make haste. O God deliver to me; make haste to help me, O Lord. Let them be ashamed and confounded that seek after my soul; let them be turned backwards and put to confusion, that desire my hurt. Let them be turned back for a reward of their shame that say "aha, aha." Let all those that seek thee rejoice and be glad in thee, and let such as love thy salvation say continually, "Let God be magnified." But I am poor and needy; make haste unto me, O God. Thou art my help and my deliverer. O Lord, make no tarrying."

When you do this ritual, lay down some white sage leaf all over your house and burn some frankincense and myrrh in a frying pan in one hand while you hold a Bible in the other. Rebuke and bind Satan in the name of Jesus and cast him into darkness where no human lives, where everything is still and dead; into another world far away from us.

Olden Days of Salem

    In Salem, in the old days they wrote on parchment paper in real doves blood, and did bonfire magic. That was how they dealt with issues their commands, either out in the woods where they had trees. And the sky and all the elements of the air or in fire places. If you confess of being a witch you will be killed and if you are accused, you will still die. By the way, before you call the powers, invoke the elements. Make sure you have all that is needed in the ritual.

To Advertise for a Husband, New Orleans Style

In the old days back in New Orleans, when a family had a daughter that needed to be wed, they would paint the front porch ceiling blue to let the people know that there was a lady in waiting for marriage as they rode by in their horse carriages.

Old Antiques and Estate Sales

When you go to an estate sale where someone has past on and you buy furniture, you may buy more than you bargained for. You can get a ghost in your house even if it is just clothing that belongs to a person that has passed on. That applies also to antique shops as well as garage sales. I went to a garage sale once and felt an old lady, about eighty five years old, outside of her house in a particular spot in the right, front side of the house. I walked up to the daughter and asked, "why are you selling the Christmas stuff?" It was summertime. She said that she didn't need them. I said that someone had died and she looked at me, shocked. She said, "Why would you say such a thing?" I then said, "Please understand. I don't mean to pry, but I am a psychic. Here is my card. There is a spirit in front of the house who is sad that you are selling her Christmas stuff. She's hurt. She is about 85 years old or so, give or take a few years." I was right. She was amazed. "She was that old. You are very good." The old man said, "What does she not want us to sell?" I replied, "The Christmas stuff. She wants to stay with you. She loves those items. She wants to spend Christmas with you." She also loves children very much. The girl said, "All right. I can keep some of the items but not all. There is just to much. There was also a wooden horse she wanted them to keep, as well. They were shocked. My husband said, "Let's go. Why did you tell them that?" I said that because I had to- she wanted me to. He thinks I should have minded my own business. I went into an antique store in McKinney, TX. The floor was moving in the front of the store with a cold draft. The floor vibrated. I brought a sales girl to fell a piece of the furniture and to feel the floor shaking. The thought that it was spooky. "What are you," she asked. "Are you a witch?" I said that I hoped I was a good one. Can you tell my future? She said to come in the back room and read for her. My husband said, "Oh, there she goes again." But when she gave me a beautiful antique lamp and some white linens, he didn't mind. But I feel that I helped the sales girl with my direction.

All About Dream Magic

Dreams can be warnings or about events about to happen. For instance, if you dream of water, it means sin. If you dream of a person who has passed, it is o.k. Just never get into a black car with them. Or for that, any car. If they call you, you should not get in. You risk your life if you do. The colors in your dream mean a lot. You should always pay attention to all of the colors, words and people. If it is a wedding, it means a funeral. A snake means trouble. A fish is luck. A sexual dream means money. You should immediately write down everything you can remember so that you can analyze it. Also, you can will someone to think of you by willing them. You can make someone dream of you. For example, I was caressed by Nick in my dream and awoke in fear. I was married to someone else at the time. I was young when I woke up. I was in my bedroom and went into the living room and said to my mother, "What time did my husband leave?" She said hours ago. I told mother that someone was in my bed who happened to be my ex-boyfriend. And what had occurred? Don't be afraid. "He was really there. Later, I saw Nick about four years later and had asked him about what had happened in my bedroom. When I was sleeping. He smiled and said that I wasn't the only one who can do things. He made a pact with someone in Central Park in New York at the age of sixteen. Guess who? Satan himself. Yes, Satan. It was for popularity and fame and beauty. Well, he got all of that but Satan tricked him. He took away other things in return such as his soul. He can be ruthless and only be nice for awhile. It becomes stronger as he gets older. His love faded more and more each year. So, the point is....you can enter dreams without the power of Satan.

Back in New Orleans, in the old days, if you had a young man who was a teenager, you had to build him a guest house in separate quarters in order to protect your daughters' repetition.

Also, the young man could not date women of other cultures. But if they were rich enough, they could go downtown where there would be a bunch of young women and only the rich could attend. If the bride bore a child, that child would become the heir of the estate.

Also, the Irish were treated like dirt when they came to New Orleans. Finally, there was this epidemic and no one wanted to rent to them or give them jobs. The Irish refused the two dollars an hour they were offered and finally got five.

The art of yoga is a very spiritual thing. It can help you find yourself. It helps you find your inner spirit and reach a higher power of spiritual awareness as well as relax your mind. It helps balance your body and align you in order to obtain spiritual enlightenment. The mental peace you'll find is tremendous. There are different levels of yoga- try the basic levels first, then enhance yourself to a higher level.

Invoking the Elements

When you call upon certain powers, be careful that you know for certain whom you are calling upon. If you are invoking a spirit, make sure it is a good one, whether it is air, fire, water or earth. Try to research it before actually doing it. It might be in your own best interest. They are very powerful and they don't like it when you toy with them. For example, if someone insults the wind, you may later hear that he or she went blind.

If a person is trying to do harm to someone, the person should say, "I bind you against doing harm to yourself and others in the white light of the far corners of the universe."

You can write your command on a piece of parchment paper in red ink or dragon's blood ink. Focus on what you are doing and burn it in the woods or in a fireplace. Sit in the Indian position and focus while you do this. Nothing else should exist this moment. Only what you see and what is real.

Self Conscious Mind
Dressing for What You Want?

The colors you dress your home with has a lot to do with your life. For example, red can be for passion. Blue can be spiritual. And yellow can bring happiness- that light, airy feeling. It also represents change. Purple is a master color. Brown is for warmth and grounding to the earth. White is peace, tranquillity and fresh flowers. Green is for money and prosperity. Clear crystals are wonderful. They help clear the air of negativity. Amethyst stones are healing and seem to help with high blood pressure. Also, purple flowers do the same. Blue and pink flowers are soft and subtle. Crystal chandeliers are wonderful. They clear and remove so much negative energy. Have you ever noticed how, when you are in a fancy hotel, the relaxation you feel when you are around the chandeliers. Marble also has a sense of peace such as floors, tables and bathrooms.

Karma

You must remember that what goes around, comes around. If you hurt somebody it will come back to you. For example, when you cheat someone, you'll get cheated on by someone else. If you steal from someone, someone else will steal from you. It's the law of averages.

You can try and justify why you did something, but that does not change the fact that you did it and you will end up paying for it in the long run. So if you owe someone money, pay them. Do not wish bad things on anyone. (I know that can be very hard to do when someone has hurt you, but you're better off leaving them to the universe). You don't have to be around negative people, because that's your own doing. Treat others as you would like to be treated. If you wish bad for someone else, ask God to please forgive you.

Some people have to mirror back their energy in order to make others stop hurting them. But try to be a very good person in all respects. As a spouse, don't violate that love, purity and respect for another because when you loose it, it's never the same again. Sometimes, people that hurt you may think that bad people are having all the fun and getting all the rewards, but I don't think so. I promise you that when it's their turn, they will get theirs. God is always watching everything. He will attend to it. Remember: he's got the whole world to deal with, one way or another. So I urge you to try to be the best person you can be, for your sake.

The Feast of Saint Ann

On June 24th, we celebrate the well being of your children. To remember her for the peace, miracles and happiness she gives to us. God bless her. We are truly blessed. November the 1st is All Saint's Day. December the 5th and 6th is Saint Nicholas. He brought peace and joy to the world. St. Jude was the saint of the impossible. Guadalupe was renowned for watching over the children. People, for thousands of years, have honored the saints to gain health, happiness and wealth. To overcome problems such as sickness, people throw feasts to honor them and get what they want. I don't think that's a good reason to honor them because you believe in them and respect them. They are God given gifts- not for you to use them.

It's funny- people seem to go to church when they're in need. Why don't they go just because it's the right thing to do? The human nature is so selfish, however, there are people of God who really believe. Those will be blessed and walk in Heaven. They don't want anything but guidance to honor God and his angels. God bless them, for they are blessed children of God. What makes me sick is when people tell you how to pray and who to pray to, when your heart is in the right place. It doesn't matter how you pray, for your prayers will be answered. People get the true miracles when they put their heart in their prayers and hope that God will have looked upon them. But, if he didn't, they love him anyway. They know that he is busy. Perhaps, he will someday answer their prayers for forgiveness when they ask for forgiveness. Some people doubt that there is a god. But let me tell you- there is for a fact. I have seen it and know it in my heart. Yours Truly, Lana. In Islam, it is customary to sacrifice a lamb for someone's health to improve. These lambs have a right to live.

Lana's Magic Garden
The Redbluff Story

I was living in Oakland, California when I recalled that my late sister Elizabeth had once told me about a town called Redbluff. My husband and I decided to drive down and have a look at the place. We wanted a place on the highway where we could put a fortune telling sign. We saw a place as we entered into the town. It was a beautiful white house set on two acres, accented with plush landscaping and a horse-shoe driveway. We looked at each other as the excitement grew within us both.

Jim was laughing. "Oh my God. It's just what I wanted" he said. "A place right on the highway and we can put a sign right in front of the house saying 'Psychic Reader and Advisor.' Oh what a place if we are so lucky to get it."

"Jim," I said, "This looks like a lot of money."

"Don't worry, maybe the landlord is a nice guy. Maybe he needs paint or carpet repairs. I can talk to him to knock down the price. I can do landscaping if he needs a gardener. If I have to do the plumbing, it doesn't matter, I have got to have this house." Jim's voice climbed to a new pitch with excitement. He smiled broad as if just winning the jackpot.

"Well, I hope you are right." I said. "But don't get your hopes too high. Keep your fingers crossed and your toes for extra protection!"

"Alright. I'll cross my legs too." Jim's excitement still radiating in his sarcasm. "Is this good enough?"

We started toward the appliance shop across the street so that we could use the phone, but Jim stopped barley out of the yard. "Susie, you go call the guy. I am watching this house so that no one gets the number." He covered the sign that said FOR RENT. I looked at him and laughed.

"What are you doing? You can't cover the man's sign."

"Ok." Jim said as he removed the paper from over the words FOR RENT, only to replace that with a pack of cigarettes and a sunglasses case. This conveniently covered part of the telephone number on the sign. "If they ask, I'll just say that I forgot my glasses case and my cigarettes." Jim looked innocently for her approval. When she did not respond, he proudly asserted, "This is my house and I want it!"

I left him there and walked toward the appliance store. "Hello." A pause. "Hello, is anyone here?" A man emerged from below the counter and proceeded to follow my footsteps into his store with his gaze. "Excuse me sir, I need to use your phone please."

"Why? There is a phone at the restaurant."

"I know, but I was wondering if I could use your phone because then I would not have to get in my car and drive to go use the phone, and then to come all the way back here. I just wanted to know if I could use the phone for a minute. I wanted to call the guy next door to see about the place for rent." The man grunted something about this being a private phone and that I needed to do my business quickly and not tie up the line. I gave him a dime for his services, and he took it the nerd. I spoke with the landlord and he agreed to come over in about ten minutes. I left quickly and quietly as not to draw any more attention.

I went outside and told Jim the good news, "Ok, the landlord is coming over. He will be here in about ten minutes."

"That's my Susie-Q. You can talk the devil into drinking ice water on a day like this." He would have continued I am sure, but then someone was walking up the drive at that moment. Jim stopped and focused his attention on the man.

"Hi. Are you Miss Adams? I am the landlord." He said

"Thank you for coming on such short notice." I extended my hand to meet his. "My name is Susie."

"And I am Jim." The man courteously leveled his glance on Jim before extending his hand to him.

"Well, my name is Mike and I am very happy to be able to show you the place today." Mike paused, but for a second too long, before continuing, "What is that? Is there something wrong with the sign?" He made a motion toward it, but Jim intercepted.

"Oh it is nothing," Jim said creating a simple diversion so that Mike would not see the sunglasses and cigarettes that still covered up part of the sign's advertisement. "Now it is hot out here. Let's go in and take a look at the place.

We wandered inside the front door and were greeted by a huge living room with a long glass showcase. Straight ahead there was another huge living room and a big kitchen immediately after that. I stood in awe at the magnificence of the architecture. We proceeded into the next room. I started rubbing my arms in pain before finally giving in. "Ooh. It is burning my arms. It is too hot in this room." I was yelling as I ran out of the room.

"I am sorry, I know that it is hot, but I have had no reason to keep the air conditioning on." Mike replied in a neutral tone.

"No, it is not that kind of hot," I said rather disoriented, but Jim had already began trying to quiet me.

He stared at me for a moment before asking, "What are you trying to do, ruin this for me?"

Mike looked at me again after turning on the air. "Are you alright?" he asked with a smile on his face that almost indicated that he was impressed with me for some reason. Mike never stopped smiling. He took us all over the house. "Oh, let me show you the big kitchen. Please notice that this house sits on a lot of land."

"I know, we saw it," I said.

"There is just one problem," Mike said without taking notice of my comment, "We only have one bathroom but there is a lot of closet space. What kind of business did you say you wanted to put in here?"

"Well, sir, my wife is a psychic and I am a car salesman. I buy and sell cars." Jim answered. "My wife would like to put out a sign where you have the for sale sign. It is perfect for a Psychic Reader and Advisor sign. Furthermore, there is plenty of parking area where I could put cars to sell." Jim stopped speaking as he could tell that Mike was visibly disturbed by this information about the cars. "I would only put a few cars for sale on the side of the house. Nothing conspicuous. They would be nice cars and not junk," Jim added to help solidify his cause.

"Why not run an ad in the newspaper that said 'Cars for sale by owner?'" Mike asked. "That is how you really should do it."

"Yes sir," Jim barked

"So you are a car dealer without a license"

"Yes sir."

"Then you probably get paid cash and don't pay taxes on the profit you make. I know what you do; I had a friend that did that. That's good money. Don't worry Jim. I'm not going to report you to the tax bureau." Mike stood still for a second thinking. "That's ok, but you have to be careful. People around here are doing the same thing. But this is a small town, and everyone knows everybody. Just be careful that you do not raise a red flag. Now let me show you the attic that I was talking about."

I went into the attic with Jim and Mike and it hurt. I felt pain. I felt torture. I felt death. I ran in and out. "It hurts!" I screamed.

Jim was now speaking to me in my language, "Shut up! Shut that mouth of yours. You are going to make me not get this house."

Mike stopped his tour and asked, "What is that language that you are speaking?"

Jim quickly said 'Greek,' as I simultaneously said 'Italian.'

"Oh, so it is Greek-Italian," Mike said as he started laughing. "You know, I am with you Susie. This place use to be an old beauty parlor but it burned down. That is why you are feeling pain and burning."

We all came down and walked back into the kitchen. Jim was signaling me to keep quiet with a closed fist, but I knew that he was only joking. "Mike, I like you," Jim says, "but I am not a rich man. I like the finer things in life"

"I see that," Mike said as he glanced in my direction. "She is dressed mighty pretty and awfully fancy. Why those look like antique clothes on her. I ain't seen a woman dressed like her except in those old 17th century movies. They sure dressed very elegant back then. Soft, the way a lady should look. Why she looks like she was made for this place. She sure is pretty that little lady."

Jim turned to me and said in my language, "Oh, he is just dying for you. I think he has a crush on you. His eyeballs are going to drop out of his head."

"Excuse me Jim, what are you saying?" Mike asked.

"Oh, I was telling her that I was going to take her to dinner after we get this place." Jim replied nonchalantly.

"So you want this place?" Mike's question was answered before he had even finished speaking. "Let me get you folks signed up. How much did you use to pay in Oakland?"

"Two maybe three hundred. It depends on the place we had" Jim said.

"Oh, I see. Well I'm afraid that I couldn't let you have it that cheap. I really must charge you more than that."

"Mike, I'll do the landscaping and I will not bother you for repairs. You do not have to put in new carpet or tiling. We will just take it the way that it is. You don't even have to fix it up." Jim was on a roll. "My wife is expecting and soon I will have another one to support. I can't afford too much because I have to save for the 'youngin' that is coming…. Isn't that the way that you country folk say it," as he slapped Mike on the back.

Mike turned and looked at Susie who was batting her long eyelashes and smiling. "I really like this place sir" she said coyly.

"Is that so?" Mike returned to Jim. "Let me see what I can do for you. Look five hundred. Two hundred for the security deposit and the place is yours."

Jim and I were mesmerized by the price.

"You think you can handle that?" Mike said as his grin stretched across his face, seemingly wider with each passing second. "Does that work for you?"

"Yes sir, yes sir!" Jim said while shaking his hand vigorously. "Yes sir, I will go and get your money. I want a five year lease."

"No problem, I think I have a lease in the car. I'll go get it." Mike was thrilled.

As Mike was walking out, I remembered that the sunglasses and the cigarettes still covered the sign. I jabbed Jim and motioned with my head for him to go and remove them from the sign before Mike were to see it. Jim walked out with Mike, who was headed toward his car. Jim walked quickly toward the sign and pulled it from the ground.

"Here is your sign." Jim said as he handed it to Mike. "I guess you won't be needing this anymore."

"Wow, you're quick. This place is yours" Mike said as he stuffed the sign into his trunk.

I joined them by the car, and innocently asked Mike, "Don't we need to fill out an application." Clearly this was a bad move because Jim began cursing me in our language. He threw up his hands while muttering; "Why God did you give this crazy woman to me?"

Mike did not take note, but rather said, "Jim, relax. You got this place. Susie, you are just a young couple. Why, I don't expect you to have credit at that age. You're in your twenties right? No, just give me the name and number of your last landlord so that I can make sure that you did not run off on him. You guys look like a nice couple. The place is yours." He handed me the key with a smile. "Congratulations" He said as he extended his hand to close the deal. Just sign here the both of you." After we signed, Mike put the contract in his front breast pocket, and looking at the house, he asked, "You got emergency contacts if one of you should get sick?"

We gave him a phone number of a family member he could reach. "Mike, thank you for everything" I said. "Shouldn't we pay you?"

"Why yes, if you have the money. I prefer cash, but I'll also take a check. You people don't look like you would write me a hot check." He stared me down in the eyes, "Would you?"

"No sir, I wouldn't do that to you" Jim stated confidently.

"One more thing," Mike said with one foot in his car, "She sure is a beauty." Nodding toward me, he concluded, "You better watch out for her in this town. They don't have women like her here."

"Mike it was a pleasure meeting you." Jim said as he hugged his new landlord goodbye. "I really mean that. You don't meet people like you very often. You are so trusting."

"You are good people," Mike replied. "Now I have to go, just leave the money next door at the appliance store. I will pick it up from there. Congratulations again" and he drove off.

Jim raced over and picked me up. "You did it!" he exclaimed. He was about to spin me around when he realized that I was still pregnant, and probably somewhat heavier that normal. He gently set me down for a quick kiss in our new front yard.

We unhooked the trailer from the Mercedes Benz that we were driving. I unpacked and carried in the small boxes of nick-nacks and linens. Jim carried in the box spring and the mattress and set them down in the living room in a corner on the right. I returned to the trailer to get the last of the pillows and blankets.

After unpacking, we went across the street to the restaurant. We sat in a booth and Jim waved to the sheriff who had just walked in. "Howdy Sheriff!" Jim shouted with his hand up in the air.

The sheriff lifted his hat in reply. "Well, howdy yourself. I don't believe I know you."

Jim gets up from our booth and walked over to the sheriff and said, "Why howdy sheriff. I'd like to introduce myself. My name is Jim, and that is my wife over there in the booth. We have just rented the little place across the street."

"Well, is that right? The sheriff looked at Jim directly in the eye without blinking. "My name is Hank. Pleased to make your acquaintance. Just what type of business are you planning on putting in there?"

"Oh, we are planning to open a psychic reader and advisor shop."

"Oh, a new psychic reader huh? I was in a town about fifteen miles from here and there is a psychic there. Her name is Doreen and her husband is Steve. They had a palm reading sign you know. And whenever they had a problem ole' Hank took care of it for them."

Puzzled, Jim asked, "What kind of problem did they have?"

"Well, you know some people go to psychics and they don't want to pay you for the reading and some want spiritual work, I think you call it." Hank stopped to hear the effect of his own voice resonating in the air. Jim was intently listening. "And some people want something for nothing. You know, wanting their money back and all. So I go over there and stick out my chest and they'd see my badge on the suit and I would assure them they needed to pay that lady because there can be no refund on services already rendered. They would come down to the department and say that she swindled them out of money, several thousand dollars in fact. Why, I wouldn't even file the complaint. I'd call up Steve, now that's her husband right, and I'd explain to him that there was a woman filing a complaint and that I'd be over to see him later." Jim still had not blinked. He was taking mental notes on this guy. Hank continued, "So Steve would give me money because I would not take the complaint. You know, he'd scratch my back, so I would scratch his. That is the way that it works around here. So if you ever have a problem, you just come to Hank. I take care of my people."

"Oh, I see sheriff. Why, I'll keep that in mind."

"You see, the people that don't take care of me, well, I don't take care of them. It is as simple as that."

"Well, it was nice to meet you sheriff. I really have to be going, but can you tell me where I can get a business license?"

"Sure, I will write it down and give you instructions and all." The sheriff made some notes on a slip of paper, and handed it over to Jim. "I'll come and visit you real soon, and we can discuss what my payroll is going to be."

"Ok sheriff" Jim said taking a step backward slowly.

"You now, you have to give me apiece of the action, if you want to work in my county. Let's call it a trust fund. You trust and we will have fun." He was smiling now.

"Alright Sheriff, give me a week and I will have it al set up by then."

"Sure, I will give you a week or two, but I will be coming to see you. Jim, jus tone more thing - keep this to yourself." His eyes narrowed as he spoke. "Understand that I run this town, and I look forward to doing business with you. Keep in mind, this is a small town, and if you don't keep this to yourself, I'll know about it. Welcome to Redbluff."

"Sheriff, I believe you are a very powerful man, and it is a pleasure to know you."

"Likewise Jim. Oh and one more thing. Where did you say you were from?"

"Oakland, California sir."

"Oakland huh? Well, I don't believe we have anyone from Oakland here."

"Well, I thank you sheriff, but I really must be going." I am anxious to get that license.

"Well you do that Jim. I will come and visit you soon."

We got in our car and started driving toward the city business license and I asked Jim, "what was all that about with the sheriff?"

He said laughingly, "He told me that he accepts bribes in case people want to file a complaint. He never lets the complaint get through.

"What a dirty dog. Was he asking you for money?"

"No, he was more or less demanding it."

"Oh no, now what?" I said to Jim.

"Relax honey, that is a good guy now."

"What's so good about him? He practically had his hand in your pocket, and you didn't even open the door."

"Well, you are only suppose to sell so many cars per year and he is a good guy because I can't get in trouble for selling more."

"Jim, you never sold that many."

"Not yet, but I plan to. With a sheriff like this, I feel mighty comfortable.

"Well, what if he wants more than you are making?"

"Baby, let me worry about that. He is a business man, and I am sure he will be reasonable."

"Alright Jim, whatever."

We rode the rest of the way in silence until we found the city license place. I went inside and left Jim sitting in the car smoking a cigarette. I walked into the office and directly toward the lady at the front of the counter. "Is this where you apply for a city business license?"

The lady nodded a faint yes before asking, "What sort of business?"

"For psychic readings" I replied.

"What is the address of the business?"

"I have it in the car, hold on for a minute while I go and get it." I ran out to the car where Jim was working on his second smoke, retrieved the address from the lease, and returned to the woman.

"Name?" the woman muttered indifferent to all that was around her. I had given her my name, and she filled in a few more lines on her own. "That will be ten dollars." She took one copy and filed it, the other copy she gave to me. "There you go."

"Don't I have to fill out an application," I asked quizzically? The woman shook her head for a no. "Would you like to see some ID?" Another shake of the head. "Well why not?" I stammered.

"We are closing. You do not need to give any ID. Will you please leave now?" The woman seemed indifferent as I thanked her and walked out of the building toward Jim and the car.

When I got in the car, I pulled the license out of my purse to show Jim.

"I am so proud of you," he said, as he bent over to kiss me. "Did they take your fingerprints?"

"No they didn't"

"Well that is funny, in Sacramento, they want fingerprints."

"Well not here. I didn't even fill out an application. Why, she didn't even want to see my ID. I could have given her any name."

"Well, don't look a gifted horse in the mouth. That's my saying. So now we have a home and a license. Lets go and turn the water and gas on."

"Well, something is just not right."

"Honey, it is fate. It is meant to be."

As we were driving through the city to see the local sights, I stared out the car window thinking about the events of the day. What a strange town. Most places give you the third degree before licensing you. Seems odd. There isn't another house for rent either. We drove through the little square as it was closing and I made a mental note that the people seemed to be acting strange. They just didn't look normal. In that I mean that they were city folks but there was something bizarre with their face. It seemed as if everyone moved about in a preprogrammed fashion. If there exists living dead, these people are the definition of zombies I thought. I shook my head back and decided that my imagination was running wild inside my head. We were almost home. Safe at last!

It was dusk and it was starting to thunder. Then it stopped and we had no storm. I couldn't imagine why we were having thunder but no storm, but it was late so I decided to just go to bed. There wasn't much to do anyway. No TV. No radio. Jim put his arms around me holding me kissing me on the forehead and lips.

"Honey, we finally got it," he said. "I always wanted a house on the highway, a big white one, and this is exactly what this is! I have a feeling we will make a lot of money here."

"I hope so," I said.

"Don't worry we will."

"Alright. Good night dear."

I rolled over and went to sleep on my side. Being pregnant, it is easier that way. He laid down next to me in a spooning position. All of a sudden we heard a loud noise and we both sat up in bed. To our surprise, it was just the automatic sprinklers in the yard. We started laughing as we looked outside at the water on the window. I was so scared that I could have peed my pants. Jim laughed and said, "BOO. Boogie man. Boooogie man."

"Stop it Jim," I said as I nudged him in the gut. "You know how scared I get."

"Yes, I know that you are a chicken shit. That's what I love about you. You are a child in a woman's body. Come here and daddy will take care of you."

"Yes dear," I said lovingly, before excusing myself to go to the bathroom.
He started laughing out loud. "And I suppose you want me to hold your hand?"

"Jim, come on. It is a big new house, and yes, I want you to come to the bathroom with me."

"Oh come on, you are a big girl. Go to the bathroom." He extended his arm
to me and said, "Take this candle with you. I will be right here when you get back."
So I go to the bathroom with the candle, and he comes crawling on the floor and sticks out his hand and grabs me. I screamed.

"It's me, it's just me." He says half laughing, half crying.

"Ugh, I, uh, my heart just jumped out of me." I said panting as I put my arms around him. "I think my heart stopped. I jumped so hard that it stopped."

"Yeah I have that effect on women."

We returned to bed and he held me as we slept. All of a sudden, here comes the thunder again, shooting at the window with bright flashes of lightning. "It is raining now Jim. Isn't it romantic?" We both love the rain. The lightning and the thunder started lifting up the flame on the candle. We slept very comfortably.

Jim had gotten up early that morning to go out and wash the car. I didn't know that though, since I was still in bed asleep. I was lying there and I felt someone grab my ankle. It was a strong grip. A voice said, "Susan. Wake up Susan." It was a woman's voice, very loving and tame.

"I want to sleep," I groaned.

"Oh Susan, wake up, you have to go to the obstetrician."

The hand kept shaking my foot and touching my back. "Alright, I am getting up," I said. I woke up and looked around and nobody was in the room. I walked into the kitchen where I noticed that there was water dripping from the sink, so I tightened the knobs. I looked out the window and saw Jim washing the Mercedes. I began to panic. If he is out there, I thought, then who is in here? I ran out of the house barefooted.

I ran to him and pleaded "How did you get out here so fast?"

He was scrubbing the car, and was too busy to look up at me. "What are you talking about he asked? I have been out here washing the car for the pat 30 minutes."

"No you weren't," I stammered.

"Yes I was."

"No, Jim you were in the room just now rubbing my right ankle, holding my right ankle, and telling me that I had a doctor's appointment."

He looked at me and said, "No that wasn't me, and that is not true."

"Jim, look at my ankle. It has fingerprints on it and it is all red. Don't tell me that you were out here all this time when you left the water on in the kitchen."

"No, I was never in the kitchen, except to go out the back door."

"Jim, you did this! You woke me up and you must have flown to get out here this fast. You were trying to scare me!"

"I swear that I didn't do that. Last night I was clowning with you. Look at the tires that I have been scrubbing."

"Well, if you didn't call my name and grab my ankle, then who did?"

"Wait here," he said, "I am going to check the house. Maybe we didn't lock the door and someone came in."

I stood outside waiting by the Mercedes while Jim went in through the back door. He checked the front door and it was locked. He looked around, but no one was there. I looked in the back door and I noticed that the water was on in the kitchen. He came back that way, shut off the water, and met me outside.

"I thought you said that you turned off the water."

"I did!" I screamed.

"Well, I just turned it off. It must be a dripping pipe. I will check it later, but no one is in the house. You are safe."

"Well how could that be?" I pleaded.

"It may have been a homeless person, and this place has been empty for a while."

"But how could that make sense," I objected. "How did they know my name?"

"It was just a dream. They would have had to come through the back door, and I would have seen them. It was just a dream. Your imagination is running wild."

"I could have sworn that I heard a voice…. Come to think of it, I heard a woman's voice not your voice. It was soft and loving."

"Oh, and she new your name? And she knew that you were pregnant too? Look Susie, you know, yesterday you started telling me that one room hurt and that it burned you, and in another room you felt death and pain. I am going to make you an appointment to see a therapist. Maybe you should speak to somebody. You have been under a lot of stress with the baby and all."

"I am not crazy, and I do not need a therapist!" I rebutted.

"I never said that you were crazy, but sometimes people need someone professional to speak to. Have you been taking your pregnancy vitamins?"

"No I ran out a few days ago."

"You should have said something. I will get you an appointment with a good doctor. I will make sure he is good. You will be needing one after all."

We put our arms around each other and walked back into the house. I went to take a shower, but when I turned on the water it looked like blood. I screamed and ran out of the bathroom screaming for Jim. He came into the bathroom with me and examined the water. "It is just rust. That is all it is. This water comes from a well, which is why it is so soft. I noticed that when I washed the car.

"Well water," I said as I tried to shake the chills.

"Get dressed so we can go and see the town."

I took my shower but as I did, I felt something stare at me through the medicine cabinet mirror. I did not want to tell Jim anymore, because he was already thinking that I flipped my lid. I went to get dressed, looking for a closet to hang my clothes up in. "Jim, look at the size of this closet," I said impatiently. It was about the size of a cloak closet.

"Uh, well just put them in another closet," he replied.

Even though it was a two-story house, I could not find any closets other than this. "I can't believe this. Whoever built this house sucks. I could have done a better job building this place. No wonder the landlord gave us this place so cheap. Sweetie, there has to be another closet. This can't be the only one."

"Look for yourself," I said.

He leaned over me and embraced my body. "Take it easy. They have these metal closets; I could probably buy one. I could just put it up against the wall. It is like a filing cabinet, but I will get you a nice one." I was about to cry. He saw my face and placed his hand under my chin and hugged me. He said, "Oh, don't cry. Let me take you out for some breakfast."

We went into town, and I went into an antique shop to browse. Jim asked the lady, an old frail woman in her seventies, if she knew of a place where he could buy some metal closets, but she was unsure of a definite answer, although she did suggest a couple of places.

"I'm going to town to check out those places. It is awfully hot outside, so if you want to stay here and browse, I will be right back."

After Jim had left, I looked around at the antiques inside. The old lady came up to me and said, "Why isn't he a jewel?"

"Yes," I replied.

"You are lucky to have a man so nice," She said. "I like your outfit. Are you going someplace special today?"

"No, I dress like this all the time."

"Really, with the gloves and the hat and all of that?"

"Yes, I love gloves," I said to inspire conversation.

"I noticed that you were looking at these. They are old ones, one of my customers asked me to sell them for her. They were her mother's."

"Well, they are nice, but they are a little too modern for me."

"Well, we have some old stick pins if you like to wear them in your hat. Some people even put them in their purse."

"No thank you," I said as I continued looking. I did buy a little hand held fan from her, which made the woman contented.

"Oh yes, that goes well with your outfit. So are you visiting someone?" the old lady inquired.

"No, I just moved into town. I rented the big beautiful white house off the highway."

"Oh that is not a house," the old lady squawked. "That is a place of business. Are you going to live there?"

"Yes, it is only the two of us," I replied. "By the way, do you know what the population of this town is if you don't mind me asking?"

She responded, "If I remember correctly, it is about twenty-five hundred people."

"I didn't see any other places for rent. I was looking after we rented that place. We wanted a place that we could live in and run a business."

"That is the only place there is to rent in Redbluff. That is why you did not see any."

I looked at her and said, "That cannot be true." There must be another house for rent."

The old lady smiled and said, "No it is true. That is the only house that you can rent and run a business as well." She continued to speak, and I listened until I felt Jim's hand on my shoulder.

"I am sorry that it took so long. I got lost. I almost forgot where I put you." He laughed. "I am so glad that I found you, I was afraid that you were lost."

We laughed together, as we walked out of the shop. We went to a phone and called the movers to send our furniture to Redbluff. Jim pleaded with the guy to bring it out right away because I was pregnant and there was no place for me to relax in our new house. The guy went out of his way and agreed to bring it the next day personally. Jim had a way of charming people into doing things they would not normally do. We went home and went to bed agreeing that we would decide where to put the furniture in the morning when it arrived.

That day, I went to the bathroom, and as I was sitting on the commode, I could feel someone staring at me. It felt as if the gaze was coming from the shower, and it felt like the presence of a dirty old man. I did not see him, but I could feel him. It felt like he had dark hair and eyes and a medium build. I went to the sink to wash my hands. I did not want to look at the water because it changed from blood to water and back again. As Jim would say, from rust to water, water to rust. I must be hallucinating. "Maybe I should see a doctor," I thought.

I approached Jim and told him what had happened. I was having hot and cold flashes, and it felt like the house was trying to talk to me.

"Now will you go to a doctor?" Jim asked as he put on his coat. "I am going to go and get some hamburgers and to find a doctor for you." He left me in the house.

I was very scared, but I stayed anyway. The house told me in my mind that it had been waiting for me, and that I could have anything that I wanted. Fame. Money. It is all yours the house kept saying, but your husband cannot stay. The baby has to go. I shook my head and put my hands over my ears saying, "This is not real, this is not real!" I ran out of the house and I waited for Jim to come back.

Jim pulled up in the driveway and saw me there. "Hi honey, what are you doing outside of the house in the driveway?"

"Just waiting for you to come home." He put his arm around me like I was having another episode. "Come inside. I got us some food. Come eat before it gets cold." We ate and I held on to him thinking, 'either this is real or I am losing my mind.'

When we finished eating, Jim stretched and said, "Let's go to sleep, the movers will be here early."

It was morning and the movers had brought the furniture. We took the beautiful cream-colored suede couch and set it down in the living room. All of my exotic silver came, and we stored it in the showcase in the living room. We put our TV in the bedroom, as well as the radio. The stereo system was placed in the living room. We were expecting the phone man to come and install the line.

"Honey, you wait for the phone man while I go scout the town for some cars to buy?"

He kissed me goodbye and closed the door behind himself. I was on the couch stretched out feeling the presence staring at me on the left. I was not sure if it was a man or a woman, and I wasn't sure that I really wanted to know anymore. I had enough of it. I then felt that there was a presence staring right at me. I heard footsteps in the kitchen. I wanted to go and use the bathroom out of fear, but I was scared of the bathroom. I looked out the window, turned my head, clasped my hands and began to pray. "Oh please Jim, please come back. They don't come around when you are here." I felt one sit down next to me, and I could see the imprint of a figure ion the couch cushion. The voices in my head came back.

"Your husband cannot stay here, the baby must die, but you can have everything that you have been waiting for."

"No, you can't have me. You can't take my baby. You can't get rid of my husband."

The voices continued.

" But we'll give you everything. You won't need them."

"No. I won't let you."

Suddenly the front door knob turned. My eyes stared at the knob-someone was coming in. Then Jim walked in. I ran to him, happy that he was back. He smiled at the door as he opened it. But as he smiled, the smile went away as soon as he stepped into the house. He put his hands around my neck, choking me. I started struggling and screamed, "Stop!" He got me to the floor. I struggled as he tried to choke me. I got up and ran to the door when I realized that he had the car keys. I ran back into the house and grabbed the keys from the floor from where we had been struggling, and I ran back outside to the car. Jim ran after me and held the car door open, frightened that I might divorce him.

"Please don't leave me. I don't know what happened." Jim was begging as tears welled in his eyes. "Please honey, I love you. I would jump in front of a car for you. I don't know what happened. Something came over me that I don't understand. It wasn't me. Please don't leave me. I'll make it up to you whatever you do just don't leave me. I'll go with you."

"Alright Jim, get in the car. We are leaving."

"Thank you," he said as he leaned in to kiss me. I was resentful, and I pulled back, but after I touched his face I knew that it was him. "I want to grab a few things before we go, since we may be gone a few days."

"No!" I was leaving. "Do not go back in that house. I am leaving."

"Please, I will only be five minutes. I will pack fast." He turned his head and moved slightly out of the way to look back at the house. As he did, he saw a woman standing out the front window. She was watching. She was transparent. She looked at him with an evil face that scared him so badly that he jumped in the car and slammed the door on his finger. It took him a moment to realize what had happened to his finger. I opened the door so he could get his hand from between the two pieces of metal. As soon as he was in the car, I hauled ass out of the driveway, burning rubber for the next few blocks. He grabbed my hand and was crying. "I love you," he kept repeating. "I should have believed you, but I just don't believe in things like this."

"Now do you believe me?"

"I believe you now."

We stopped at a Denny's to get some water. It was still very hot outside. "Where are we going to go?" I asked. I was crying and almost hysterical after fully understanding what had happened.

"Give me the keys. You are in no condition to drive," Jim said.

"Ok, but don't go in the direction of the house."
We drove all night with no breaks until he said, "There is a gas station, we should stop and fill up."

"NO! They are after me. Do not stop." I was crying and pleading. "Please keep going. They are behind us."

"No they aren't" he said. He held my hand as I cried, "Easy, easy, you re ok now. You are going to lose the baby. You are so nervous, and if you keep crying you might trigger a miscarriage. You have to calm down. He put the radio on very softly to distract my mind and calm me down. He was holding me with his arm around me as he drove past. "It is going to be alright."

I told him that the house wanted to kill him and the baby. It started to storm, and we couldn't see the road any longer. We ran out of gas. We pulled over in front of a house, which was off on a dirt road. It was raining hard, and he ran up to the door. An old lady answered. "I am sorry to bother you at this hour, but my wife and I ran out of gas. She is pregnant. Is there a gas station around nearby, or can I use your phone to call a cab?"

"Why don't you bring your wife inside? All the gas stations are closed, and they will not be open until morning. I will make you some hot tea, and we will see what we can arrange" The old lady smiled as she went back inside.

I was sitting on the couch crying and shaking, as the old lady looked me up and down. "I think she is traumatized," the old lady said. "What has happened?"

Jim looked at her and said dryly, "You might think we are crazy, but we are running from a place that is haunted and she said that the ghosts wanted to kill the baby. She did not want me to stop and get gas because she felt like the y were still behind us." Jim blinked to signal that he had finished speaking.

"I'm sorry. I shouldn't be crying like this and shaking, but I really just can't help it." I said still quivering.

The old lady took charge. "Here's some hot tea. Go on, drink it." She went into the kitchen and retrieved some Frankincense and some garlic, in which she crushed them together and gave them to me. "Chew on this," She said. "It is a home remedy."

"But I am pregnant."

"It won't hurt you," the woman said. I chewed on it, but it tasted terrible.
She watched me slowly chew, and finally stated, "Swallow it." I swallowed it, as Jim tried to get directions to the nearest motel.

"It is late, and I know we are keeping you up," Jim was saying. "Do you think it is possible to get a reservation this late?"

"I don't see why not. I will go and wake my son and have him drive you." The old lady returned a few minutes later. "My son is asleep, and I do not want to wake him." She paused, and then said, "I'll tell you what, I have an old motor home out there. Why don't you and your wife go and spend the night out there? I will get the key."

Jim said, "Oh, that is awfully nice, but we do not want to impose like that on you."

By this time I had stopped crying and shaking, but it still took me another ten minutes to thank the old lady for all of her services and generosity. "I don't know what you gave me, but it made me stop shaking and feel sleepy. Thank you."

"Please take the key to the motor home and sleep there. We can discuss this in the morning."

"Thank you," said Jim. "We will accept."

She took us out to the motor home and said good night to us. "Get to bed it is late," she said.

"What time is it?" I asked

"Twelve thirty. Good night."

We locked the door and I fell into a deep and relaxing sleep. We woke up late in the afternoon. We went to the lady's door and I hugged and kissed her as she made us coffee. "I want to thank you, for I don't know what I would have done without you."

"That is alright," she said as she kissed me back on the cheek. I was all wrinkled up since I had slept in my clothes. I was embarrassed by my appearance, and I apologized for my looking so rough.

The old lady sat down and began asking us questions. "What town are you from? What was this place? Tell me about it if you want."

I looked at her, and said, "You know, it was so late last night, that I did not even get your name."

"Galie."

"You don't have a husband," I said.

"He has passed on."

So, I explained to her about the house and what was happening. She inquired about the name of the town and we told her that it was Redbluff. Her eyes widened at the mention of this.

"You know something about this place don't you?" I asked.

"Yes I do. There is a psychic a few blocks down the street, and she has been trying to get a license for ten years. She has hired an attorney, and from what I understand she could not get a license there. There are other psychics that couldn't get a license either." The older lady sighed feeling that she had done a great service to those other psychics.

"Excuse me Galie," I said. "Is that the way that you pronounce your name?"

"Yes."

We continued discussing the situation as her son walked in for lunch. Jim immediately stood to introduce himself. "Oh here you are, my name is Jim. What is your name?"

"Tony."

"You mother is very nice. She let us stay here." Jim announced.

"Yes, she told me," he said rather indifferently. "I want to take you to the gas station. I have a gas can that you can use. Come on I will take you there now."

I stayed and talked with Galie as the men left for the gas station. I learned more about the mysterious town of Redbluff. It turns out that the house that we moved into was once a funeral home. A lot of psychics have rented the place, but they never stayed more than two nights.

"The place is haunted you know." Galie said as she straightened the lines of her dress.

"I don't know," I replied innocently.

"I have never seen the house, but I can describe it to you. I have heard so much about it over the past ten years. I'll tell you how you got your license so easily." Galie said as an air of mystery engulfed her.

"How Galie," I asked mesmerized by her logic.

"Because the house was waiting for you."

"Oh my God!" I looked at her and put my hands over my mouth.

"You were very lucky to get out. You must not go back there. I will tell you what to do." I stared at her unable to move as Galie dictated the answer. "You must leave all of your belongings in the house."

"Oh, I will not go back. I will send the movers to get all of our furniture. I am not going near that house. I will hand them the key and they'll go in there and pack everything and bring it to me."

"That would not be a good idea. Now listen to me Susie. I have a lot of angels around me that protect me. I'm part Indian you know."

"You look it."

"I know a lot of things that my Mother and Grandmother and Great-grandmother taught me."

"Who are you?" I gasped. When she explained who she was, I knew that I had heard her name before. It was too familiar to me. She was my late sister's step mother in law. The one that had sent me to Redbluff. "So you are Pete's mother?"

"No, step mother. I married his father, but it did not work out. After my husband died, I was lonely for somebody, and he was there. He wanted different things in life than I did, so we parted as friends." She sighed. "He was a good man, but just not for me."

"I see." Taking this in, I returned her to the matter at hand. "You were saying that I can't get my clothes or my furniture out."

"No you must not, because they can enter into your clothes. They will even enter into your furniture. They will come after you. Don't you find it strange that the lady down the street could not get a license, and you can get one in less than half a day?"

"Yes, I found that strange."

"I know what I am talking about. Just let it be. You should be happy that you got out alive and safe." She looked at me to make sure that I understood. "You are safe now." Her eyes widened. "Go tell the lady down the street that you have a license. You do have it with you I suspect?"

"Yes. I was going to get a frame for it and put it on the wall but I didn't have a chance."

"Let me see that," Galie said. "Yes, it sure is. Go show the lady down the street. She is on the left hand side a few blocks down. You can't miss it; a little house. Show her this license and she might want to buy it. That way you can get back some of the money that you have lost."

"Alright. I'll do it." I said rising from my seat. I walked down the street until I came to her door. I looked at it for a moment, and then knocked.

"Hello. Did you come for a reading?" The woman at the door asked.

"No, I am a friend of Galie's. She sent me here. May I come in and talk to you?"
She looked me up and down for a moment before inviting me in.

I entered and sat down in the first chair that I could find. "I understand that you have been trying to get a license for the city of Redbluff for fortune telling."

"That is right, but there is not a license to be had."

"Oh, but there is," I said.

"Really, how? I've checked with attorneys, and I know that the city does not issue them because it is prohibited."

"No, I have one." She looked at me with squinty eyes before asking me to leave. "I really have one. Look, I will show it to you." I reached out and handed it to her. She sat mesmerized holding the license and looking at me.

"How much did this cost you?" She snapped.

"Ten dollars."

"How did you do it?" The lady pleaded.

"I just went up there and the lady at the desk handed it to me and told me to pay ten dollars. I got it in less than ten minutes."

The woman became very frustrated at this news. She stood and began pacing while muttering obscenities to herself. She finally turned to me and said, "I've been trying for ten years with lawyer appeals trying to get the license and I couldn't. But here you come waltzing in off the street and they just give it to you for ten dollars." She handed me back the license and said, "I'm busy. It is time that you run along."

"Listen, I am not here to rub this in your face. Galie told me that you wanted a license, and I have lost all of my belongings and all of my money. Galie thought that you might want to buy it." I looked at her with puppy-dog eyes. "I will even give you the house that I rented, although I do not recommend that you stay in it. It is haunted!"

"How much are you asking for the license?"

"I don't know. Let me think," I said.

"Well, you do that and let me know."

"How about three hundred?"

"I have spent over five thousand with lawyers. That really is a deal." She went to her purse to get the money, but then she stopped still bent over her bag. "I will have to check with my husband, but as far as I am concerned the three hundred is yours. She returned to me and continued, "That is a 290% profit, but it is worth anything to me."

"Alright then. I will be right back," I said getting up to leave.

"I will cancel all of my plans. You promise you will be back?"

"Yes."

I walked back to Galie's house and noticed that Jim had already returned. I discussed selling the license for three hundred dollars. "We only have a hundred left," he said. "We're almost broke." He put the gasoline in the car and we went over there immediately. We walked up to the door, and again knocked.

"Oh you came back rather quickly."

"Here is the license, as promised," I said as I extended it to her. She handed me the money, but I quickly noticed that she tried to short change me by fifty bucks. I handed the money to Jim who counted it immediately.

"There's only $250 here."

"Oh, I am sorry. I thought that I had given you $300." She went back to her purse to get the other $50. She gave it to Jim and we quickly left.

"Some people.... Let's go back to Galie's, I want to give her fifty bucks for letting us spend the night. She is such a sweet lady." We knocked on the door and expressed our gratitude. "We sold the license and we wanted to give you this."

"Oh nonsense. You kids lost everything," said the old lady.

"No, seriously this is the least that we can do for you for helping us. Please take it," Jim said.

"If you want to do something for me, promise me that you will never go back to that house. I know that your furniture as well as your pillows and blankets are still there. You are going to be tempted to go back, but please promise me that you won't go."

"But Galie," Jim stammered, "It's over three thousand dollars in furniture, all of our clothes, pots and pans; everything we own is in that house."

"Jim the silver, that's another fifteen hundred," I said.

"Oh yeah, that's right," Jim said.

"I don't care if it was ten thousand, it's not worth putting you and your wife at risk." She grabbed Jim's arm and pulled him close. Looking deep into his eyes she said, "Listen to me I warned you now, you must heed what I say. Don't go back for you are in great danger. That house wants your wife. Don't you understand. No one could get a license for ten years, and she got a license just like that," as Galie snapped her fingers for effect. "The house was waiting for her. Look how your wife dresses." Galie's voice was shrill with sincerity. "She dresses like she's from the seventeenth century, and the house is from the same age. Think about what I'm saying. You've heard it from the other psychics, and she couldn't get a license. Don't you understand that the house drew you there?"

"Ok Galie, you made your point," Jim said to her. Together we got in our car and started driving back to Oakland. "We have to go back and talk to the landlord and try and get our money back since we were only there for a few days." We drove in silence for a few more minutes before Jim exclaimed, "He's just got to give us our money back. Maybe we can sell him the furniture."

"Yeah Jim, but what about all of our clothes? What if the old lady's right?"

"You know I don't believe in the supernatural." He paused, "But after I saw her with my own eyes, I believe her now. Either way we're going to need to get maternity clothes for you."

"But we can't go to the house Jim."

"Okay, we won't. We'll find a phone in the city, and I'll ask him to meet us somewhere."

Mike met us and we explained that we were afraid to live there because the house was haunted. "Well I should just sell the place," Mike said as he handed them a few hundred dollars as a refund. "Sorry I can't give you all of your money back. I've never personally seen any ghosts but former tenants have complained of the same thing." Mike laughed at himself and said, "I don't need no boogie man comin' after me once I show the house." We thanked Mike for all of his help and went searching for the former owner of the house.

We found the owner, an Italian, and he told us that his father was not a religious man. The owner was heavy set with dark eyes, an olive complexion, and a cruel temper. He was a dirty old man who always ogled at the ladies and used a lot of foul language. His mother by contrast was a strong Catholic, she was the sweetest woman you'd ever meet and she love people. They're both deceased; his mother died from a stroke in the house, but his father died in a hospital. His father, who was part psychic, was always on the dark side. The upstairs bedroom was his and when his parents died he inherited the place. He needed to pay the taxes so he rented it out, and it became a funeral parlor and mortuary. He sold the place though because of something that could not be explained. As it seems, two twin boys would haunt that place during the services.

We offered to sell our furniture that was left in the house to the owner, but he wasn't interested, neither was Mike. We went to the antique shop in the town square and offered it to the cute old lady who knew so much about seventeenth century fashion. The old lady refused to make an offer without seeing it first. We were too scared to enter the house so we told her she could take it with the manager's permission at no charge. We left and went back to Oakland. We were free of the spirits, but disappointed since we had barely enough money to start over. I didn't do readings for two years after that. I guess I was scared.

The End

Lana's Magic Garden
"Lana's Home"

Lana was living in Plano, Texas, where her dog, Sheba had nibbled a small child. Sheba was half Irish setter and half Collie and Lana always called her the "Friday night special." She also called her a redneck. Lana loved her dog since it was a puppy. They bought it off a street corner in North Dallas. She teased the dog, telling her "your mother went sleeping around, you're a mutt."

Unfortunately, Lana's lease on her apartment was revoked because Sheba was becoming a nuisance. She pleaded with the manager to let her stay, but he would only give her a month. She had to find a new place immediately. Poor Lana fretted and worried about moving. Where would she go on such short notice? What about the money for a new place? How would she find a place big enough for her stuff, her 4 children and for Sheba? Lana started to look hard. She found houses ranging from $1300 to $2200 a month. Lana really wanted to buy a house but she knew that after she paid the moving company to pack and move she wouldn't have enough money to purchase the house, and it all had to happen in a month! That was just cutting it too close.

Thankfully, during her search, Lana came upon a sign in a yard of cute house in a nice neighborhood: "FOR LEASE." She pulled the car over and she and the girls piled out.

"Look girls, isn't it beautiful?" asked Lana, tearfully.

Monique swelled with pride because she was the one who spotted the house first and told Lana to pull in to check it out.

"It's fantastic. Look it's got white carpet inside," said Monique, with her nose plastered to the window.

"Sheba can even have her own back yard!" Chanel yelled.

Suddenly, the look of hopeful happiness drained from Lana's face. "What if can't have a dog? What if the landlord doesn't allow pets?"

"Don't worry." comforted Monique, rubbing her mother's back.

The girls ran excitedly from window to window, sneaking peeks of all that lay beyond the walls of their house. While they were running around the house, choosing which rooms would be their bed room, Lana found a lock box on the front door with a phone number on it. She pulled out her phone and dialed the number. It rang once. It rang twice.

"Hello?" a voice asked softly.

"Hi, I am standing on the front porch of your house for rent and I was wondering if I could take a tour of the inside. I am very interested in renting it." Lana was so excited the words just rushed out as one big sentence.

"Very well. It is $1300 a month, but you are in luck. The landlord reduced it to $1200 today. It's a four-bedroom house with two baths and two living rooms, a patio, a back yard, and a two-car garage. Does that sound like a good deal?" the voice asked.

"It's perfect!" Lana accidentally shouted into the phone.
The voice on the other end cleared their throat and continued, " There's a number for the lock box to get inside. Use the key inside to take a tour of the house and call me back if you are interested."

Lana thanked the voice on the other end of the phone and hung up, repeating the numbers to herself so she wouldn't forget them. She tried and tried again to open the locked box with the house key, but it wouldn't budge. Frustrated, she picked up the phone and hit redial. She asked what the number was again and found that she had been putting the wrong number into the lock box. After receiving the correct number, she thanked the old lady and hung up. Just as she was about to try out the new combination, she heard a truck pull up into the driveway. A gypsy man stepped out of the driver's side and asked how much Lana was asking for the house. Lana informed him that she didn't own the house and was actually thinking of renting it for herself.

Now faced with a competitor, Lana had a problem. She left her glasses at home and couldn't read the combination the old lady had given her. She decided to ask the gypsy for help, on one condition.

"You can come in the house and view it, AFTER I do, if you help me to open the lock box," stated Lana. She was sure he wanted the house to move in a dozen families. Gypsies were like that, you know.

The man agreed and the four of them walked into the vacant house. It was freshly painted and had new carpets. The girls continued tearing around the house shouting, "This is going to be my room!" , "No, Chanel, I'm going to have this room!" , and "Mom, come check these rooms out!!"

Then, the question Lana dreaded, "So, do you know how much the landlord wants for this house?" asked the gypsy man.

Lana sighed, " They were asking $1300 until today. Now it's $1200."

The man nodded and smiled.

"Look," Lana gushed, " you can't have this house. I am not trying to be pushy but I've been told to I have a month to find a new place to live by my apartment manager. I have dog he doesn't like and that's why he's throwing us out."

The gypsy raised his eyebrows, "Is that so?"

"Yes," Lana practically shouted. "I'm desperate. Please, we have to have this house. He's going to throw us onto the streets."

"Ok lady, ok. I understand. You did see the house first. Thanks for letting me have a look anyway. You can have the house, I won't call," he lied. And he left.

As soon as he was gone, Lana picked up her phone to call the realtor that she'd talked to earlier to accept the house, but the line was busy. It was busy for her entire drive back to Plano. Finally, she got through. Lana asked if she could come tomorrow and fill out the paperwork for renting the house. She told the old lady about the gypsy man that had been out to look as well. The voice on the other end told her that a man had already called her, a roofer named Johnson. He wanted to come that night to fill out paper work but the lady said, "I didn't like his voice. He was a bit dodgy. If you want the house, come now!"

The old lady realtor gave her directions to the office and Lana and the girls jumped back in the car and zoomed over. When they arrived there were two women in the office. Lana said hello and introduced her daughters. The two women commented on Monique and Chanel's French names and inquired whether they were French or not. Lana filled out the application and paperwork for her soon to-be-dream home. As she passed the application fee to one of the women they informed her that she'd, "know something within a day or two."

When Lana got home that night she told her husband everything that had happened to her and the girls that day. She told him how wonderful it was and did he want to see it before they actually moved in? He informed Lana that he trusted her judgment and "I'm sure it's a wonderful house," he cooed.

Lana called the realtor back wondering if they'd let her lease to buy. The two ladies said no and told her she'll know whether she passed the application process by 5:00 pm tomorrow. They also told Lana that even though she had excellent credentials they were a little worried about putting her possibly putting a PALM READING sign on the doorstep. Lana gathered they weren't too fond of psychics. She assured them that wouldn't happen.

As soon as they got the word, Lana and her husband, Nick, hired moving me to start packing their belongings. They were so excited, moving into such a great house for so cheap. As they were packing and the movers were moving, the doorbell rang. Sheba started barking loudly as Lana walked to the door. She hissed for Sheba to shut up when she saw who it was. The dogcatcher waited outside the door until Lana opened it, giving Sheba a kick to keep her quiet.

"Hi, I'm investigating a story about a little girl being bitten by a dog. You have a dog don't you?" asked the dogcatcher.

Lana could see the little lady in the blue suit standing on her doorstep was from the Animal Society and not the pound. Lana figured the best way to deal with her was flattery. As a psychic, Lana often knew people's weak points. She commented on her beautiful complexion, flashy suit and movies star looks. After she buttered her up, Lana answered innocently, "No ma'am, I do not have a dog." Because, by this time, Sheba had been shoved into the back bedroom and the radio was on covering her barking.

"I do believe," Lana said hesitantly, "that I did see a dog. Well, there are a few dogs on this side of the building, I mean, the man upstairs has a Losa Opsa."

"No. No," interjected the little blue suited lady, Ms. Johnson, "This was a big dog like a Shepard. It was fully grown, reddish blonde color…."

"Yes, I do remember seeing that dog hanging around a little while ago," muttered Lana as Ms. Johnson took a step toward the door. "Oh, do forgive me, I'd invite you in but we are moving and the house is a mess."

To keep Ms. Johnson happy, Lana gave her directions on how to find the 'reddish-blonde dog' she was looking for in the other apartment building, far away from Sheba. As she walked Ms. Johnson to the corner of the building with the flowerpot, Ms. Johnson confided that she hoped she didn't really find the dog. "If we find this animal, ma'am, we will have to put it to sleep for biting the little girl. And, if it has rabies, then they'll have to cut it's head off and too all kinds of tests on it after it's dead. It's sad, really," sighed Ms. Johnson.

With that Lana parted ways with Ms. Johnson and returned back to the apartment to finish moving. She explained to Nick what the little lady in the suit had said about putting Sheba down if they found her, all the more reason to get out to the new house and quickly. With Ms. Johnson still in the area, Lana and her husband decided it'd be best if they snuck Sheba out as quickly as possible. They ran her down to the car, threw her in, and covered her with a blanket. She kept poking her head out from under the blanket and Lana knew they were close to getting caught. Lana shoved Sheba's head down and started singing her favorite song: "Two Irishmen, two Irishmen, digging in a ditch. One Irishman said to the other Irishman, 'you dirty son of a bitch!" She could see the dog roll her eyes and knew that Sheba was thinking "you're nuts, lady!"

Lana's husband stayed with the movers while Lana drove the dog out to the new home. As they pulled into the drive of the new house, Lana leaned over and ruffled Sheba's hair and whispered, " I love my Sheby, Eeby, Heeby because your aren't bad. You didn't bite that little girl. She shouldn't have been holding ice cream out for you, right?"

The girl's mother wanted to get a few extra bucks off Lana because she knew Lana made her money as a psychic and she didn't care if the money came at the expense of Sheba's life. The girl's mother caused more problems as Lana's family moved out of the apartments. She called the manager and complained that no one was doing anything about the bite her daughter had received. Lana tried to get her deposit check back and the manager refused citing the dog bite as a reason to keep the money. Lana argued with manager, trying to explain that Sheba never bit the little girl. She licked ice cream off her hand. The little girl came with a scratch that could have come from any of the three cats that lived in her own house. Lana explained to the manager that she tried to give the girl's mother a check if she would just release the apartment complex and Lana of any liability. The girl's mother refused. Lana even paid the woman $250 if she would just drop the whole thing and take the girl to the doctor to get her checked out. Finally the girl's mother agreed. She'd take the money and write a letter absolving the complex and Lana from any wrongdoing and liability.

Lana's manager still wouldn't return her check. Until she showed him the letter the girl's mother wrote. "Why is this so hard for you to believe?" she shouted. "Just look at the letter and give me my deposit!" Finally, the manager agreed and handed over the check.

The next day, Lana received a call from the girl's mother. She demanded more money, another $100. Lana reminded her of their deal for $250 and that was all she was going to pay. She knew the woman hadn't taken her daughter to the doctor to get a check up. She knew that the girl's mother was going to use the money to buy more drugs. "You don't need to be in that environment," said Lana. "You're a good mom, but you need to get away from that boyfriend and those drugs. What are you going to do when child services comes sniffing around and finds all that marijuana? Do you want them to take away your daughter?" With that, the woman hung up.

Now, that Lana's problem with the neighbor was cleared up she could get back to helping her family get everything else unpacked. She had just started opening boxes and placing things around her new living room when the phone rang.

"Hello?" Lana said.

"Hi, Lana, I need a reading immediately!" It was a young client of Lana's.

"I would love to help you, but I'm just moving into my new house and I haven't found all my things to do a proper reading. Can we schedule it for next week?" Lana asked.

"NO! It's very important, Lana," her client said nervously. "I must come now!"

Lana asked Nick if he would mind her leaving the unpacking to do a reading for this frantic young woman. He replied with, " It is very good luck for you to have a customer before you can even get unpacked. Do not turn her away. We'll help you find your cards."

Lana uncovered the phone and said, "Ma'am, come on over. We can do it this afternoon. I'll see you in a little while."

"Thank you, I'll be there in 45 minutes," the girl gushed.

When she arrived, Lana ushered her into the reading room filled with boxes at the back of the house, so as not to be disturbed. "Have a seat," she said, gesturing to a box next to a table.

Soon after, the reading was over and the young client left. Lana packed up her reading things and left with Nick for the store. Because it was just down the road, Lana left the girls in the house with Chanel in charge. The girls were playing in the different rooms of the house when Monique heard Lana calling her, "Monique, come here. I need your help." Monique left her play spot to go find Lana, but became confused when she couldn't find her mother anywhere in the house.

"I'm over here, Monique," the voice whispered eerily.

Monique ran smack into Chanel when she rounded a corner, following the voice. "Chanel, I keep hearing mom calling me but I can't find her. Do you know where she is?"

Chanel stared at Monique like she was crazy, "She's not home, idiot. I saw her leave with dad an hour ago." She rolled her eyes at her sister.

Monique's mouth dropped, "That can't be. She was just talking to me!" The girls all gathered together and went from room to room to prove to Monique that Lana wasn't home and that the car was gone from the driveway. Just when they got to the window facing the driveway, they heard it. "Monique, come here!" the voice hissed evilly. This time all four girls heard the voice and tore off for the safety of the living room.

A few moments later, Lana and her husband returned from the store. They walked in to find the girls huddled together in the living room, faces frozen in fear. "You look like you've all seen a ghost," Lana smiled. Her smile faded as she looked from Monique and Chanel to Jeavante and Doreena and asked, "What's wrong? What happened?"

The girls all started speaking at once. Lana caught the word ghosts and scary voices and she chuckled. "No, dears, there isn't anything in this house. You girls were just letting your imaginations run wild. There is absolutely nothing to worry about. Your father and I are here," she said reassuringly as she hugged her husband. "Let's finish unpacking and get our beds set up so we have somewhere to sleep tonight, okay?"

Everyone agreed and they set about unpacking. Soon it was time for bed. The girls were in their pajamas and ready for bed. Lana and Nick were very excited. This house was the first place they'd ever lived with the master bedroom on the other side of the house. It was the first chance Lana had to be intimate with her husband in years. Now that they were alone, Lana could hardly wait to get her hands on that man of hers. Then there was a small sound outside the door. Lo and behold, there stood all four of the children, holding their blankets and pillows tight. "Can we come sleep in here with you? We're scared," they all chimed together.

Lana chuckled, "Girls, you will be fine. Daddy and I are just down the way from you. You have your very own bedrooms. There's nothing to be afraid of."

"Pleeeeeeease?" The girls wailed.

"Oh, all right," sighed Lana.

The girls bounded into the room, blankets flapping out behind them. Lana threw her husband a look that said "not tonight honey." He laughed and tugged the girls up onto the bed with him.

The next day, the family finished unpacking and setting things in their rightful places. Lana, hoping for a bit of romance that evening, gave her girls things to do after dinner. That should keep them busy, Lana thought to herself. She sent Monique, Chanel, Jeavante, and Doreen off to bed and headed to her bedroom. Lana slid out of the bathroom, the aroma of rose perfume trailing after her. She winked at Nick, lifted the covers on the bed and slid under them just in time to hear a knocking at the bedroom door. Frustrated, Lana moaned and threw the covers over her head as her husband went to answer the door. There stood the girls. Lana was furious. She was tired of this childishness. Nick was better at convincing the girls they'd be ok after he heard their story about more voices in their rooms. He told them to stay out in the living room for the night, that way they'd be closer to him and Lana and not on the other side of the house.

"Dad, we can't sleep in there. We hear footsteps," whispered Chanel in a trembly voice.

Lana poked her head up from under the covers and looked at the girls. "We are never going to be alone tonight. Might as well go see what's going on," she sighed, "even though I've told you all before that there is nothing in the house."

"Well, let's go look, shall we girls?" answered their father.

They all inched out into the hallway together, straining their ears for any hint of a noise that sounded like voices or footsteps. It was quiet as a tomb. Then, Lana's husband shoved them all back into the bedroom, "I want everyone in our room!" he whispered.

"What is going on?" demanded Lana as the girls toppled through the doorway on top of her.

The girls father shot Lana a look that turned her white and stopped in her tracks. "I will tell you in the morning," he said severely. "Let's all curl up on mommy and daddy's bed and get to sleep," he cooed to the frightened children as he winked at Lana.

There were hugs and kisses all around and they started to nod off to sleep. Lana had a nagging feeling that the information her husband was keeping from the girls wasn't going to be good. Lana leaned over and kissed him good night. All together they heard the girls making kissing noises and Chanel, who was totally disgusted whispered, "Ewww, they're kissing. I bet they don't even care if the ghosts get us."

"That's all they ever do, smoochy, smoochy," added Monique.

The next morning everyone woke up and finished the last tidbits of unpacking. The girls were preoccupied when Nick pulled Lana aside. He had a grave look on his face when he told her what happened the night before. "I think that our house is haunted, honey. I heard footsteps in the hallway and someone wailing. I have also heard voices up in the attic."

Lana was horrified. Why didn't she hear anything? She was the psychic one. Why hadn't she experienced the footsteps and wailing? "We must bless this house immediately!" she whispered urgently.

Over the next week, Lana busied herself with the cleansing of all the items in the house, all the rooms in the house, even the carpets. She performed the cleansing until she was satisfied all evil was removed from the house and her family's possessions. Soon after, a woman came to Lana for a reading. During the reading a dark haired, middle-aged woman appeared in the reading room. Apparently the apparition only appeared to Lana's client because the only thing Lana experienced was the front and side doors banging open and closed repeatedly.

"Lana! There's a woman, dark hair, b-behind, y-you. I think she's a ghost!" stuttered the woman.

"Impossible. I would know if there was an entity behind me. That's why I'm psychic," shouted Lana over the banging doors.

"I'm telling you, she was there! She just vanished in the blink of an eye!" shouted Lana's client a little too loudly.

For at that moment, the banging doors stopped and she and the client were screaming at the top of their voices. "She was smiling at me, Lana, while she stood behind you. Then she vanished, POOF! Just like that."

By this time the whole family had rushed to the reading room wondering what on earth could be causing such a racket. Monique flew through the doorway out of breath just in time to hear the description of the lady. "That's the ghost!!" she gasped.

Lana dismissed the nonsense because she didn't see the dark haired woman and she thought the banging doors were nothing more than a draft grabbing the doors and swinging them back and forth. Nothing happened in Lana's house for a long time after the appearance of the dark haired woman.

About one year later, Lana finally admitted that she'd felt something follow her from the hallway into her bedroom. She lay down on her bed, feeling terrible. She knew it was a supernatural entity following her around the house. Lana finally started closing the doors behind her every time she entered a room. One day, after being followed down the hallway, Lana walked through the doorway into her room and closed the door. Immediately, she heard someone trying to open it. Lana tiptoed to the door and flung it wide open, hoping to catch the culprit. No one was there. The hallway was empty. She shut the door and went back over to the bed. The noise started up right away. Someone was definitely trying to get into the room. Lana stayed put on the bed and noticed that soon, the noise stopped and she heard footsteps walking away from the room.

A week later, Monique came to Lana complaining of hearing the voices again. "Mom, the voice is talking again. She sounds just like you." Monique was scared.

Lana became concerned. Now she had experienced the ghost and it was tricking her daughters into thinking it was she. Finally, she went to Nick. "We must do something about this, don't you think?" she asked.

"Do you want to move out of the house?" he blinked at her in disbelief. He knew how much Lana wanted this house in the first place.

"No, I don't want to move. I can't think right now. Let's go out for dinner. I'll grab the girls," Lana got up wearily and started calling for the children.

That night, at Furr's Cafeteria everyone was stressed. Lana was most stressed. She loved that house and fought hard for it. She fought the gypsy, the apartment manager, and the mother of the girl who was bitten. No ghost was going to run her out. "If those ghosts want to play, let's see if they can handle what I throw at them," said Lana defiantly.

"Excuse me ma'am. Did I just hear you say you have ghosts in your house?" a meek little cashier questioned Lana. Lana didn't realize that she'd been talking out loud when she went up to pay the bill for dinner.

"Yes, you heard correctly," Lana stated, eyeing the cashier. "I am a psychic, perhaps you've heard of me. I'm Lana." She shook hands with the little cashier.

Lana told her a brief version of what was plaguing them at her house. She told the cashier how the ghost mimics her voice to confuse her four daughters. Lana also told the cashier, now wide-eyed, how the ghosts follow her down the hall to the bedroom and how Nick tries to scare them off, yelling in a booming voice " Leave my family alone!"

The cashier handed Lana her change and wished her good luck in ridding her house of the meddlesome ghosts. Lana rounded up her family and headed back to the house.

The ghost kept up their antics over the years. They no longer performed only for Lana's family. They scared Lana's clients and family friends. One particular time a friend of Lana's who was going through a divorce came to spend time at the house. She showed up on the doorstep and walked right, wanting a place to put her suitcase. Reluctantly, Lana told her she could share Monique's room. The next morning Lana asked her guest over breakfast how she'd slept.

"Everything was great. Slept like a log. Except you should probably have a talk with that daughter of yours, Monique. She kept shaking the bed and whispering silly things in my ears all night," said the guest, completely unaware that Lana's house was haunted.

Upon hearing about the bed shaking and whispering, Lana promptly spit coffee unexpectedly out of her mouth. She glanced at her husband, worried. What were they going to do? After assuring her guest she was fine, Lana helped to clean up the mess. Fortunately, Lana's friend, Shirley, had decided not to burden her loving friends another night. She decided to stay in a hotel, and started to pack up her belongings when Lana asked her husband, "Do you think we should let her stay in a hotel? That's not very hospitable."

"Yes, Lana but what if she discovers that it isn't Monique shaking her bed and mumbling in her ear. What are you going to tell her then?" he suggested.

Lana eyed him suspiciously, "What do you mean? Do you think we should tell her about the ghosts?"

"I think should tell her we have them and if she wants to stay she is more than welcome to. But you should tell her the truth if you tell her anything," he commented as he walked out of the kitchen.

Lana ran up to Monique's room to tell Shirley everything and offer her the room to stay so that she wouldn't have to go to a hotel. Unfortunately, Shirley was already asleep. It's only half past 9pm, thought Lana. The next morning Shirley came down into the kitchen to face a nervous Lana and family. "How did you sleep last night, Shirley?" Lana asked nervously.

Shirley laughed, "Oh fine but that girl blabs something awful in her sleep. Poor Monique, you should get her to a doctor."

After a jab in the side from Chanel and Monique, Lana decided it was time to tell her friend Shirley about the ghosts in the house. Lana reached out for Shirley's hand and said, "Shirley, I have something to tell you. You know you are always welcome, being a great friend of the family, and you can stay as long as you want to" Shirley smiled and looked around at all the faces, wondering what was going on.

Lana gathered all her courage and held her breath for a second. She let it out slowly, "That wasn't Monique wailing and mumbling last night. She wasn't shaking the bed either."

"Of course it was," tittered Shirley nervously. "Who else would it have been?" She looked around the room, waiting for an answer. Her gaze landed on Nick.

"Shirley, Lana has something very important she wants to tell you and you must remain calm," he smiled as he poured some coffee. He passed the coffee to Lana and smiled.

Lana took a breath and blurted it out, "We have ghosts, Shirley, in that bedroom. We believe it is an old woman named Kathryn that died a long time ago. She's the one that shakes the bed."

Mouth hanging open in disbelief, Shirley stared. "You're joking, right?"

Nick's smile faded, "No Shirley, it's not a joke."

Immediately, Shirley stood up, walked out of the kitchen and into the hallway where her bags were sitting. She grabbed the two bags and looked up at Lana and Nick, "Thank you, Lana, but I'll be going now."

And out the door she went.

Nick and Lana burst out laughing, "Do you think we scared her away, girls?"

Monique, Chanel, Jeavante, and Doreen giggled loudly.

"At least she and the good doctor won't get a divorce now," Nick said between gasps of laughter.

"How do you figure that, dear?" asked Lana.

"Well, after sleeping in bed by herself that was haunted, she'll jump in bed tonight with the doctor and they'll get everything settled!" Nick said matter-of-factly.

From then on, Shirley only came to visit in the daytime and never spent the night at Lana and Nick's home. They did have lots of visitors though. One year at Mardi Gras, Lana's nephew Rick, spent the night. He woke up the next morning and said, "You've got ghosts, you know that?" He left the next night. Lana's family became quite used to the ghosts. By 2002, Monique and Chanel wouldn't leave the room. Lana would scold them daily, "Leave that poor old woman alone!"

"We're playing with her, Mom," they'd shout back.

Nevertheless, nowadays Lana and her family keeps the house very clean, so as not to offend the entities they share it with. They also found that the cleaner the house the better fortune seemed to smile on them. They mowed the grass and kept the garden clean and money came pouring in. Proof positive that if you take care of the house, it will take care of you.

Some time later, Lana researched the history of the house and found out a minister used to live in it. It was haunted then. There's a rumor the real entity occurred and someone paid the newspapers to keep it secret. One of Lana's houses is about ten miles from Plano, Texas. That explains why Lana got the creeps in Plano. She couldn't stand it, she says. Lana and her children still live in the little haunted Texas house. The ghosts keep them company since Lana's divorce and help out with readings when her clients arrive.

The End.

Lana's Magic Garden
"Pots and Pans"

My aunt told me, "Be careful of strangers and watch your luck." She and my uncle were living in London, England. One day, they went to a small town about 20 miles away to have lunch and shop. My uncle and aunt came home with the shopping bags, laughing and in a good mood as they walked through the door.

Their daughter had loaned two pots to a new neighbor who'd come by while her parents were out shopping. He knocked and asked the daughter to loan him a cooking pot or two and he'd return them as soon as he was finished. Before the daughter could answer, the neighbor barged through the door and headed for the kitchen. He started grabbing pots and pans out of the cupboard. He finally settled on a pot the young girl handed him.

When my uncle learned that their neighbor burst through the door and took pots from the kitchen, he was outraged.

"Why does he have to take my pots? The nerve! Doesn't he have the money to buy his own pots?" bellowed my uncle.

"Oh well," sighed my aunt, "They are low-lifes. Maybe he will return it when he's finished." She rolled her eyes about her head. "Maybe they will invite us for dinner."

Time passed, and my aunt and uncle had a huge fight and my uncle ended up moving to Madrid. My poor aunt was completely heart-broken, and took to drinking. Her business as a very famous psychic was faltering and the house was no longer full of hopeful people, trying to learn about their futures or connect with loved ones. They would even fly from different countries to hear what my aunt had to say. My aunt was so alone and missed her husband terribly. She hated being in the house alone. She became more and more vulnerable as the days went on.

The neighbors still came to borrow small items and always promised to bring them back eventually. My aunt noticed, however, that since her husband had moved to Madrid, the neighbors came over frequently to take her kitchen things. It was almost as if they wanted to take advantage of my aunt's vulnerability. They'd come to borrow dishes, more pans, tables and chairs, and even the vinegar and black pepper from the cupboard.

Finally, my aunt confronted her neighbors after struggling with suspicious thoughts for some time. She went next door with a wagon and asked for her tables and chairs, pots and pans, and pepper back. She had to hold her nose while she spoke because Nick-with-the-pocked-marked-face smelled awful. He and the old man, Larry, crowded around my aunt making snide remarks about her figure and her clothes. Theodore and the very fat Matilda stated they would return them tomorrow. My aunt knew something was wrong when she received a glare from Theodore's wife as she hissed, "You will never get the pots and pans back!"

My aunt pushed past Theodore's wife, full of rage, and started slamming her pots and pans into the wagon. Next she grabbed the vacuum cleaner they had taken hostage for a few months. She threw the pepper and one of the chairs in the wagon and with all the strength she could muster, my aunt turned on her heel and marched back to her house.

She was so angry with Theodore's wife. She determined the unfortunate Theodore wasn't such a bad man, but his wife was full of greed and had an evil soul. My aunt, being a powerful psychic, knew all about evil souls. She could remember something she heard once from my uncle's grandfather: "Never live near paupers! Their bad luck clings to you and tarnishes your good luck." Now, my aunt would change her luck from the bad string of events back to good luck by reclaiming her pots and pans from her evil neighbors.

My aunt put all her belongings back into the house and, within a few weeks, had calmed down. Soon, after reclaiming her possessions, a wealthy client of my aunt's appeared, wishing for a reading. My aunt hadn't had visitors since her husband left and saw this as an opportunity to get some help retrieving the rest of her tables and chairs. Her friend agreed and loaded the tables and chairs into his pick up truck. The following day, my aunt started her "bad luck exorcism." Everything needed a good scrubbing. The drapes and floors were washed, the bathroom was scrubbed, and the pots and pans were washed down to cleanse the house of all the bad luck.

With her good luck restored, my aunt decided that she would try and get my uncle to come back and live with her. She once described her family as a lock and a key, a lock will only hold one key, and the lock and key need to stay together. She set off to find him and was shocked when she did. The poor man was near starvation and if she'd wasted any time in finding him he would have died. They had a bite to eat and my aunt convinced him to return with her to the house. She had left the children who were 15 and 8, alone and wanted to return their father to them.

Everyone at the neighbor's house tried to fall into the old routine of borrowing and cursing. Since my uncle's return their plans never went as smoothly as they had in the past. No one could ruin the love my aunt and uncle had. Their love and good luck was too strong. The terrible neighbors next door couldn't hurt what my aunt and uncle had. They were even more outraged when they realized that my aunt and uncle still had more money, they were still living in middle class society, and they wouldn't loan their pots and pans to the vagabonds living next door. My aunt recounted to her husband everything that had happened to her in his absence. She told him how the terrible paupers next door would cook in her pots, cursing her with poor business. She told him about the vacuum that stayed in their possession, causing her to drink large quantities of alcohol.

My uncle remembered all these events and told me about them years later. "It is very important you do your own cooking and watch whom you allow into your home," he said. "The pots are special. You feed your family with the food you prepare in them." He leaned forward and whispered, "Meat equals money. The paupers cooked in your aunt's pots and pans to curse us. The neighbors wished evil upon us to ruin our happiness, take our home and our prosperity."

"How did they curse your pots and pans?" I whispered, wide-eyed.

"Ah," he winked, "they use the spoons and, hitting them against the borrowed pots, call the spirits into the pots and pans. It causes the luck of the pot's owner to change."

Thankfully, my aunt and uncle regained all their possessions, good luck and prosperity, but I warn you to be careful of strangers wanting to borrow your pots and pans. Beware of the people less fortunate in luck; they may try to steal your good luck.